Twenty Twenty-Four

Robert Durward

First published in Great Britain in 2017
Copyright © 2017 Robert Durward

A CIP catalogue record for this book is available from the British Library.

Published by Robert Durward
Printed and bound in Great Britain by Clays Ltd, St Ives plc
Typeset using Atomik ePublisher from Easypress Technologies

Hardback ISBN 9780995771116
Paperback ISBN 9780995771109

Dedicated to;
Sandra, Colette and Nicole

Table of Contents

Introduction

To join me on this journey, imagine if you will that this book was written and published in 2024. It owes much to futuristic fiction, both utopian and dystopian, but it is not a novel. There are no imagined characters, no dialogue, no focussing on the affairs of any one person or group of persons. Nor is it a formal history, stuffed with references and footnotes. There is no focus on the details of policy, no costing of alternatives, no effort to deal with objections. Rather, we look back together at crises of the past and use their lessons to transit to a new order for the future.

I hope you will gain much from this book. I do not expect you to agree with all that you find. Perhaps you do not share my view of the world. Perhaps, even if you agree that my view of what will happen, you will find what I regard as a future world on the edge of utopia as a world on the edge of nightmare. More likely, you will simply disagree with my opinion of where things are heading and how they can be overcome. If this is the case, you will find me in partial agreement with you.

Talking about the future is often a precursor to looking like a fool. However obvious it may seem to us, nearly everything that happened in the past was unexpected at the time. I am not aware of anyone in 1639 who believed the Stuart State was about to collapse. Nor do I think anyone in 1788 predicted the occurrence or course of the French Revolution. The course of the Great War repeatedly took all the clever men by surprise. The difficulty with looking ahead is partly that most of the facts are unknown, but partly that the facts already established will be seen out of focus. We always tend to see the world through the twin lenses of unreasonable fear and of wishful thinking. For the world as it is, facts already established provide some certainty. For the world as it may be, the only certainty is to wait and see.

I have lived for rather a long time and observed a great deal. This has not given me a crystal ball, just a better than average ability perhaps to look ahead. In business the farther ahead of the curve you are the more success you enjoy, in politics, slightly ahead of the curve you are regarded as gifted, too far ahead you are labelled insane. I am content to let others be the judges of that one.

My starting position is that Britain, along with the majority of the free world, is cursed with a destructive system of political and economic governance. Except by accident, our parliamentary democracy does not put the best people in charge or recognise the will of the majority. It does not even produce consistency of government. It may have come close to this at various times in our past. After all, to live in a country no more imperfect than the one we have, we must have been doing something right for some of the time. But it does little that is right or good now. It enables rule by unrepresentative factions, aided and abetted by a client media, to plunder our nation, and to buy votes with the change. Not surprisingly, we are where we are.

And where are we? Well, over the past twenty years, our rulers have piled up a mountain of debt. In every year of this time, I have wondered – *can this continue?* How much longer can we keep adding billions and trillions to the mass of our public and private debts? The answer so far has been that we have continued adding to the mass. But we have been living in a fool's paradise. Like a man who eats and eats until he weighs thirty stone; every morning he wakes up, crawls from his bed and says to his shaving mirror: *"There you see, I am still alive what idiots those doctors are with their nagging!"* Sooner or later, that man will fall down dead. Sooner or later, that mountain of debt will crush us. It will never be paid off. The creditors must eventually be disappointed. Long before they are disappointed, though, every lying promise our politicians have made must be broken, and uncounted millions who have worked and saved and hoped for a better future will have been impoverished and enslaved.

And debt is not the whole of our problem. We have a public sector that looks after its own people ahead of those it is paid to serve. We have an approach to the regulation of private business that slows the economic growth on which our lives depend. We also enrich well-connected business interests at the expense of small and medium enterprises. Our energy and environmental policies are a joke. They are based on a set of unverified but easily falsifiable claims about climate change, and on a belief in "renewable energy" alternatives that are as yet nothing more than wishful thinking.

Or there is the systematic immorality of our foreign policy. Ever since the end of the Cold War, we have been turning parts of the Third World upside down. Scarcely without exception, where we have invaded, or merely intervened, we have made worse. We have sent servicemen, who joined up to defend their country, overseas to kill civilians. Or employed them to sit in air-conditioned rooms, to kill at the press of a button. All this, and we have not made ourselves any safer. We have done worse than that. We have raised up terrorist threats that would have shocked observers from the Northern Ireland of the 1970s. We have set in motion waves of refugees that dwarf the movement of peoples that ended the Western Roman Empire in the fifth century. We have ignored, or at best feebly resisted, the growth of new threats from Russia and China. We have allowed large parts of the world to suffer under murderous despots that no civilised order should tolerate.

I do not believe that this state of affairs should be allowed to continue. More to the point, I do not believe that it *can* continue. There must come a day when the whole rotten edifice of how we are ruled will fall to the ground. I do not say that this will happen without pain. To return to the image of the fat man, heart attacks are painful and dieting is hard. But, given that the collapse is certain, we have both a need and a duty to confront the question of how we are to reconstruct our world to the benefit of ordinary people, here and in the world as a whole.

We need a new kind of democracy, to give us the leaders we need and that our children deserve. We need a new approach to taxation and the delivery of public services. We need a new system of foreign policy. In short, we need a new world order.

To end as I began, I do not expect you to agree with all that I say. But do join me in exploring how a day of reckoning that cannot much longer be delayed might yet be turned to our advantage. If we do not give serious thought to these matters, we shall make it all too easy for extremists and dark forces, already at work, to prevail.

Robert Durward, Quarrymaster, Lanark 2017

Chapter One – The Gathering Storm

George Orwell wrote his famous dystopian novel *Nineteen Eighty-Four* to highlight the danger of allowing the state to grow out of control. Derided by many at the time, the book proved uncannily prescient. What he envisaged was a world that was split into competing ideological blocs where alliances change, seemingly at a whim. But now BIG BROTHER IS WATCHING YOU, via CCTV, Facebook, Twitter, internet tracking et al. Strangely enough, it was the people who imposed much of this surveillance on themselves. Anyone stepping out of line is met with a storm of criticism on the worldwide web on a par with the Two Minutes Hate. But here on Airstrip One, or Britain as we still call it, the clocks have not yet struck thirteen. Thirty years have passed since 1984 and it would appear that Orwell's only significant mistake was timing; it is now time to look into the future again...

2015: A Conservative "Victory"

The Conservative Party won the 2015 General Election by a slim majority of just twelve seats. It gained twenty-four seats by the use of high-tech voter profiling in marginal constituencies and a remorseless attack on its former Lib–Dem coalition partners. However English voters who were fearful that Scottish Nationalist MPs could hold a hung parliament to ransom also played a big part in the Tory victory. Indeed Nicola Sturgeon had actively played up this possibility as she wanted them to win. She had figured out that a Conservative Party in power at Westminster would give her free rein to play on the Scottish bitterness that remained long after Thatcher had gone to strengthen the vote for separation.

The implosion of the Labour Party along with the Conservative Party in Scotland, not to mention the collapse of the Lib–Dems, indicated much deeper problems with the political system. Perhaps the most significant aspect of the 2015 general election was people voting to stop things they didn't want to happen rather than being able to vote for the things that they did want. The English did not wish to be dictated to by the SNP, the Scots no longer wanted Labour and few wanted Mr Miliband as prime minister. The majority of people in the UK were now effectively disenfranchised with a staggering 76% of the electorate not having voted for the government of the day. We had tired of political parties squabbling over the same centre ground or swinging destructively from left to right and then back again. We had also wakened up to the fact that our democracy had fallen into the clutches of professional charlatans and instinctively wanted to punish them.

The Sham of Representative Democracy

The bloody French Revolution that lasted until 1799 had sparked the British people's appetite for more power. Not wishing to suffer the equivalent of the guillotine, Britain's elite began to contemplate this possibility. However it was not until the Chartists formed in 1836 that a movement to gain power for the people actually began to take shape.

The *People's Charter* called for six reforms to make the political system more democratic:

1. A vote for every man twenty-one years of age, of sound mind, and not under-going punishment for a crime.
2. The secret ballot to protect the elector in the exercise of his vote.
3. No property qualification for members of Parliament in order to allow the constituencies to return the man of their choice.
4. Payment of members, enabling tradesmen, working men, or other persons of modest means to leave or interrupt their livelihood to attend to the interests of the nation.
5. Equal constituencies, securing the same amount of representation for the same number of electors, instead of allowing less populous constituencies to have as much or more weight than larger ones.
6. Annual parliamentary elections, thus presenting the most effectual check to bribery and intimidation, since no purse could buy a constituency under a system of universal manhood suffrage in each twelve-month period.

Apart from annual elections, the Chartists' demands were eventually met but not until almost a century later with the Chartists disbanded and with blood having been shed. However, 'votes for all' turned out to have been a Pyrrhic victory and the fledgling electorate fell victim to snake oil salesmen. Rather than electing the best people to represent them, they derogated responsibility to political parties instead. These were organisations that would seldom work in their best interests but prove useful to blame if anything went wrong. Since then, a great deal had indeed gone wrong but this flawed arrangement turned out to be so disempowering and addictive that it had become set in stone. Convenient perhaps, but our abrogation of responsibility along with power had started the clock ticking on a very big bomb indeed. For a political party to retain power, it had to constantly prove that it was more deserving of support than all the other parties put together. Given the five-year electoral cycle, this meant short-termism, slanting information and offering 'incentives' in return for votes.

Although most MPs entered politics with every intention of making things better, the more talented and enthusiastic they were, the more frustrated they became. Some gave up altogether, some persevered or simply had nowhere else to go, but few were happy in their work. Although their primary duty was to their constituents, few dared defy the whip. Not only would their chances of promotion have evaporated overnight but they would also have faced demotion and possible withdrawal of their party affiliation. Draconian sanctions such as this could not be used in the private sector without due process. Although they could have continued to sit as independents, very few ever did. Even with 650 top notch MPs, under the party system, they would still have been set at each other's throats in a vicious battle to preserve their careers. The House of Commons was by now more akin to a gladiatorial arena than a respected base for democracy. As a result, few dared enter and the majority of MPs, including Prime Ministers Blair, Brown and Cameron, had never held significant positions outside the political bubble.

In routinely bribing voters to gain power, politicians had created high-expectation client states living well beyond their means. However, with austerity continuing to bite, voters were getting restless. To seek revenge, or perhaps even to wreck the system that had marginalised them and made them poorer, people began voting for anti-establishment extremists such as Trump, Corbyn, Le Pen, Sturgeon et al. Political parties were hoist by their own petard but we were all going to get caught in the after-burn. The prospects of a happy ending were fading fast as paper currencies, government bonds (IOUs) and quantitative easing lost their charm as stocks and commodities were inflated far beyond their worth as a hedge against fiscal collapse.

Beneath a Mountain of Debt

General elections had become 'bribe-fests' to buy votes and the pigeons were coming home to roost. Problems ranged from having to borrow £2.5bn per week, an unaffordable public sector, a black hole in Treasury-raided pension funds, growing nationalism in Scotland and an inability to deal with dangerous international developments. The migrant crisis had continued to worsen since President Putin had become actively involved in Syria but the EU restricted itself to squabbling about immigrants rather than tackling the problem at source. The politicians knew they would be dammed whatever they did so chose the safe option of kicking the problem into the long grass instead. However the long grass was getting shorter and something was going to break soon.

The Conservatives claimed that they were the only party able to protect the nation's finances but the national debt had doubled under George Osborne. They had also promised to get the annual deficit down. Under Gordon Brown, it had peaked at £160bn in 2009–10 and George Osborne claimed to have reduced it to less than £100bn. But the deficit is only the difference between what the public sector spends and Treasury receives from taxes. It is not how much the government needs to borrow to pay all its bills. The overall national debt continued to climb from £760bn in the 2010 financial year to £1,500 billion or £1.6 trillion in 2016, a debt unprecedented in peacetime.

The Chancellor claimed that the public sector deficit as a proportion of gross domestic product – or the total market value of all the goods and services produced by the economy – had stabilised. However, this deficit does not include many long-term liabilities, such as pensions and money raised for the National Health Service or other government bodies to pay for capital projects using private finance initiatives and pension funds. By now we were already racking up almost £1bn per week to meet interest payments. So far Britain had been remarkably fortunate in being able to borrow money at a low rate of interest. February 2016 saw a major collapse in global share indexes triggered by America's attempt to raise interest rates, big problems in China and the collapse of oil prices from +$100 per barrel to sometimes less than $30. Bizarrely this led to ever cheaper borrowing for the British government as investors rushed towards safe havens. Even Argentina became attractive to those with large amounts of cash as it had already been bankrupt and looked to be on the way back. Swiss banks had been charging depositors to hold Swiss francs since the crash in 2008. Depositors were in effect betting on the Swiss franc gaining against the other major currencies and it duly began to rise. However the Swiss government didn't want an inflated franc as it would have damaged their export markets and Swiss banks bought huge amounts of euros to dampen down the franc. Those looking for a safe haven and income had been stiffed. Some 'safe' government bonds also went negative meaning that lenders were paying borrowers to take their funds in the hope that their capital would be in safe hands. Safe perhaps but steadily diminishing as the effects of inflation eroded its eventual buying power. It is said that 'those the Gods wish to destroy they first drive mad' and the economic madness of the early twenty-first century was a certain sign of impending destruction in one form or another.

Other problems were waiting in the wings to propel national debts from their misleading and simplistic 'percentage of GDP' interpretation to an 'insolvency index'. Greece's position in the Eurozone had not improved. The Mediterranean countries – particularly Greece and Italy – were inundated with immigrants from the Middle East and Africa, putting an additional strain on their already fragile economies. The poverty-stricken Mediterranean countries were having to protect their richer neighbours to the north from the consequences of their failed foreign policies. Germany had tried to alleviate the pressure by promising to take as many refugees as wanted to come. But this backfired spectacularly with Angela Merkel's party losing heavily in local elections. While some Germans welcomed refugees with open arms, others protested that there were only so many newcomers the country could support. Extreme nationalist groups received a boost, refugees were attacked and the open border Schengen agreement came under increasing pressure.

Mediterranean countries on the frontline lost no time in pointing out that Germany seemed to be more prepared to spend money on Syrians and Eritreans than its fellow Europeans. However, the German government's hands were tied as the Constitution Court in Karlsruhe had already questioned the legality of the European Central Bank's quantitative easing policy of buying an unlimited number of government bonds as the Eurozone crisis worsened. It even lodged a complaint with the European Court of Justice which duly found the ECB to be in breach of EU law.

As the prospects for the Eurozone worsened, the UK government claimed that the British economy had turned the corner. Some economists agreed; some didn't but they always did cherry-pick the statistics to prove whatever point they wished to make. The reality was grim. With the Eurozone being a major export market, problems there would drag the UK down as well. The ECB's bond-buying programme – officially known as Outright Monetary Transactions – had by now pumped so much money into the weak economies of the Eurozone that inflation soared. At long last the central banks spotted the iceberg ahead and began to raise their interest rates. However, fearful of causing an adverse reaction, these were limited to a maximum base lending rate of 3%. Low perhaps in historical terms but this represented a six-fold rise for those who had become accustomed to base rates of 0.5% or less since 2009.

The sharp rise in interest rates reduced consumers' ability to borrow and choked off any hope of recovery. Rising interest rates also dissuaded industry from investing in capital projects. The downturn on the high street hit businesses the length and breadth of the country. The lack of money meant even less opportunity for young people entering the jobs market. Graduates flipped burgers as those desperate for work often lost out to a black economy strengthened by over-regulation, not least Living Wage regulations. Few youngsters could now afford to leave home as the housing market had also become disconnected from the real world. Rather than being bought by home seekers, many houses had become investments for people looking for safe havens for their cash or rental income to augment their poorly performing pensions. Young people starting out could not compete in a housing market dominated by wealthy retirees, mostly from the public sector.

Brexit: A Spanner in the Works

As people looked around for someone or something to blame, they settled on the EU. This caused fresh fractures between the Eurosceptic and Europhile wings of the Conservative Party. It was clear that the in–out referendum would solve nothing. The negotiations over the UK leaving had produced little of substance, merely dividing the Conservative Party even more than before. Referendums seldom settle the unrest they generate as the losing side always wants to have another go. The SNP were already demanding another vote on independence in the event that the UK chose to leave the EU. Little did they know their bluff was about to be called.

By now, Labour had a very big problem indeed. In an attempt to make the party more democratic, Ed Miliband had opened up their leadership elections to the membership. Once Corbyn's name was on the ballot paper, Labour's fate was sealed and he knocked out his opponents in round one. He was even helped by some Tories who had paid a £5 joining fee simply to vote for him. Corbyn may have been mild-mannered and quietly spoken but his views made him a vehicle for the ideologically-driven hard left to recover old territory and they swiftly swung into action. They began by taking over constituencies then moving people they saw as Blairite to the side or getting them to resign. In desperation, all the front bench non-Corbyn supporters resigned in mass and triggered a vote of no confidence. This was simply ignored by the party hierarchy. Corbyn was left leading a rump of left-wing diehard loyalists but by now he was unstoppable. Parliament was riven with intense factional fighting on all sides, weakening its ability to foresee, let alone deal with, the approaching storm.

Then came Brexit taking the political elite by storm, even its supporters had only faint hopes of succeeding and the Leave campaign had been anything other than a joined-up effort. But that didn't matter, the people had at long last been given the chance they had been waiting for and were determined to rock the boat as hard as they could. In the financial markets, there was a collapse in confidence and sterling plummeted. With Britain set on leaving the EU, several large international banks warned that they might to move their headquarters away from London and investment dried up. Money was being stuffed into anything that looked reasonably safe; gold, property, fine art, antiques and wines all benefited with scant regard to the prospects of ever selling them again. So far only pre-shocks had been felt from the tectonic plates but the pressure was growing.

Within a few short days, the prime minister had resigned and the Conservative Party, which had also opened up its leadership elections to the membership, faced their own version of the Labour Party meltdown. Boris Johnson was seen as the natural successor to Cameron but he was a Marmite character. Loved and loathed in equal measure, danger loomed. His 'close friend and ally' Michael Gove then claimed that Boris was simply not up to the job and threw his own hat into the ring. This caused a media firestorm which reduced both men's campaigns to ashes leaving only Andrea Leadsom to challenge Theresa May. However, by this time the men in grey suits had decided that this was no time to tear the party apart and Leadsom was persuaded to withdraw leaving the way clear for Theresa May to become the new leader of the Conservative Party and prime minister. May lost no time in firing David Cameron's closest ally George Osborne and declaring that austerity would be put on hold until the economy recovered sufficiently. The main Brexiteers, along with Angela Leadsom, were rewarded with ministerial posts. Political patronage was once again used to quell opposition and the rebels fell silent. However, by this time, the tectonic plates really were starting to grind and the new prime minister would be powerless to reverse a process now gaining momentum throughout the West. Brexit initially had more effect on mainland Europe than at home where the stock market rapidly bounced back. Sterling did not recover fully but that helped the balance of payments and exports. Other EU countries began contemplating leaving the EU whilst they still could, if they still could. The common thread now holding the EU together, especially the Eurozone part of it, was debt. All of the Eurozone countries were now heavily in hock to the European Central Bank which was in turn financed by Germany and Germany did not treat its debtors lightly. Greece had acted tough but was quickly forced not only to toe the line but accept EU technocrats calling the shots in Athens. What had started as a noble venture to prevent war between its member states had turned into de facto defeat and occupation by Germany, albeit that had not been Germany's intention. The architects behind the EU project knew all too well that monetary union without political union was impossible but they were prepared to wait their time until a federal states of Europe became inevitable. They might even have got away with it if they had avoided rolling out their common currency when the world economy was headed for such a massive slowdown.

Scottish Troubles (1)

Following Brexit, the Scottish nationalists claimed that as Scotland had voted Remain, a second referendum would be required. The Scottish result did not actually provide major support for the separatists as only 40% of the Scottish electorate had voted remain with over one million voting for Leave, including four hundred thousand of the SNP's own supporters. The opinion polls showed that the majority of Scots still wished to remain in the UK and the nationalists were reduced to making the usual empty threats. Although the Conservative majority in the House of Commons was still wafer thin, the SNP were by now attracting widespread public opprobrium by trying to use this to further its own narrow cause. They had everything going for them in 2014 including a publicly-funded but highly partisan white paper called *Scotland's Future* which was sent to every household in the country. However by 2016 the vast majority of Scots realised that it had been a cynical fabrication and were now a lot more sceptical of the nationalists' claims. Just as Portugal, Italy, Greece and Spain, the so-called PIGS, were bound to the EU by their debt, Scotland was bound to the UK. Its 2016 £14.8bn deficit required HM Treasury to send almost £300m north every week just to keep it going. Rather than acknowledging the realities of their predicament, diehard nationalists simply claimed that Scotland needed its own currency to become truly independent. However, this would have been impossible without a lender of last resort and no one, apart from the UK, would fund this level of borrowing with no prospect of ever getting repaid. Westminster had no option but to fund Scotland as, if it had gone down, it would have taken the rest of the UK with it. Although some in the EU might have accepted Scotland as a member – to gain revenge for Brexit – they could not afford another Greece. Spain and France were implacably opposed to an independent Scotland becoming a member of the EU in any event. The SNP realised that the game was up and was reduced to sabre rattling to keep their supporters happy.

The Chickens Come Home to Roost

Theresa May claimed to be winding up the economy but there was little that she could do as the Bank of England armoury was sadly depleted by previous episodes of quantitative easing, and for many the misery continued. The one beacon of hope for the Conservative Party was Jeremy Corbyn, who easily saw off the challenge for his leadership, by Owen Smith, in September 2016. The Labour Party was once again following the same path to electoral obscurity that had taken it to the brink of disaster in 1985 when Neil Kinnock, in the speech of a lifetime at party conference, managed to turn the tide. However, Momentum was now in too deep to be dislodged and even the once disgraced Militant member and Trotskyist Derek Hatton was soon to be welcomed back into the Labour fold. This was of course completely unrelated to him having made millions from dodgy property deals and being a fan of Jeremy Corbyn.

There appeared to be no option other than soldier on in the hope that it would eventually all work out for the best. The only 'growth industries' now were public sector strikes, food banks and protest marches against austerity. Meanwhile local authorities continued to protect their jobs and pensions whilst cutting much-needed public services.

With tax revenues dropping dramatically, more cuts were needed. But public sentiment prevented any trimming of the failing NHS. Within government, departments battled ferociously to defend their budgets and the fractured and fractious Parliament did not have the political clout to lay down the law. Not only was the 'smack of firm government' sadly lacking but the lightweight nature of Britain's MPs, most of whom had never had to deal with a real crisis, in Parliament or anywhere else for that matter, became painfully obvious. People watched in despair as ministers dashed from one meeting to the next, issuing vacuous and misleading statements along the way. Yet another lesson not to be forgotten.

By now the Treasury was avaricious and the private sector was increasingly being taxed into extinction. The top rate of tax headed towards 70%, though there were some baby boomers around who still remembered the Beatles singing:

Let me tell you how it will be.
That's one for you, nineteen for me…
Should five per cent appear too small,
Be thankful I don't take it all.

In their song *Taxman* from 1966, they were complaining about a top rate of taxation that had reached 83%, plus 15% supertax, making the marginal rate for the wealthiest 98%. Consequently, the Beatles, the Rolling Stones and other bands moved offshore.

In an effort to reduce the tax bills of some of their wealthier clients, some smart accountants and even HSBC had set up bogus schemes when New Labour came to power in 1997. The most notorious of this genre began in 2004 when Gordon Brown gave special tax concessions to the film industry. Hundreds of high earners, including former Manchester United boss Sir Alex Ferguson and ex-England managers Sven-Göran Eriksson and Glenn Hoddle were among investors who paid £2.2billion into one such scheme. The plan was a complex process to buy and rent back Hollywood blockbusters to studios. One such scheme, Eclipse Film Partners No 35 LLP, bought rights to Disney films such as Enchanted and Underdog before sub-leasing them back to the studios. However, HMRC obtained a High Court judgment to have the schemes wound up. Tax officials began issuing punitive penalties of up to twenty times the amount invested. Someone with a two hundred thousand pound investment could expect a tax bill of between two and four million pounds with only ninety days to come up with the cash. Many celebrities claimed that they would go bankrupt and stories circulated of people even committing suicide. Needless to say the accountants and banks behind the schemes held on to their fees.

The Treasury then really began scraping the bottom of the barrel and mounted a raid on job perks such as health checks, gym memberships and mobile phone contracts. Workers had been allowed to forgo part of their salary in return for certain work benefits. Companies warned they would be forced to scale back free medical checks for staff, undermining attempts to keep the country healthy. However, their pleas fell on deaf ears and these allowances were also scrapped.

Once again, with tax rates climbing, the wealthy saw no reason to stay in a country where the taxman took everything he could lay his hands on.

Banks were by this time loaded with cash that they couldn't lend, as the criteria for lending meant that borrowers practically had to prove that they could manage without it before a loan was approved. Commercial and private borrowers were therefore being denied the working capital that they needed to progress.

Meanwhile pressure from the Corbynite left for nationalisation without compensation meant that investment faltered. Few believed that Corbyn would ever become prime minister but no one was willing to bet against another Labour government that would almost certainly be hard left. Few would risk putting money into a UK project if there was the slightest chance that a socialist government would confiscate it via nationalisation.

Police numbers had also been cut which quickly led to a reduction in the number of crimes being reported or pursued through the courts. However, behind the scenes crime levels were actually rising and anyone with money or property had become a target for cash-strapped legislators as well as crooks. In light of the growing body of disaffected youths with few prospects and little stake in society, there was potential for serious trouble. However, the really big crimes were going on behind closed doors. A number of traders, kicked out of the City following the downturn, came up with ever more sophisticated financial scams. These were so complex that when – mostly on the off chance – their frauds were uncovered, the trials had to be conducted by experts without a jury.

Old-fashioned bank robberies were a thing of the past. The bankers were the robbers now and the mobsters who used to run the streets turned to cybercrime which proved far more lucrative. Even HMRC was raided and lost countless millions to professional hackers. Human ingenuity was more than a match for any computer. No one could feel safe whether their cash was under the bed, or in a formerly hallowed institution.

In November 2016 Tesco Bank revealed that an unprecedented attack on its customers' online accounts had resulted in the loss of £2.5m. Like many other scams of this nature, the fraud was perpetuated at the weekend when security staff were harder to reach. Such was the confusion that Tesco initially reported that 20,000 accounts had been affected although this was later revised down to 9,000.

Andrew Bailey, the chief executive of the Financial Conduct Authority, told the Treasury select committee that *"there are elements of this that look unprecedented and it is clearly serious."*

The National Cyber Security Centre, a recently created division of the surveillance agency GCHQ, confirmed it was working with the National Crime Agency in an attempt to track down the fraudsters but they were never identified. In its defence the NCSC claimed that *"in the case of cyber-related incidents, it can, on certain occasions, take a significant period of time to understand the incident given the technical complexities involved."*

However, Conservative MP Chris Philp, a member of the Treasury select committee, told the BBC that it could have been the work of a foreign power. *"I don't think we can at all rule out the possibility that this is state-sponsored."* Although the prime suspects for this type of activity were normally Russia or China, North Korea was also now launching highly-sophisticated cyber-attacks against its Western enemies.

Skilled people, entrepreneurs and the young were leaving the country in droves with many heading east to the New World as well as the more traditional destinations of America and Canada. Economic migrants and refugees fleeing war zones were no longer our only problem. The physical composition of the country was being materially altered as the indigenous population was replaced by others. That said, the public were now becoming more concerned about emigration than immigration with so many skilled and qualified people heading out. The 'brain drain' gathered pace and parents could only watch in dismay as their children and grandchildren fled to far-flung shores. The NHS now had great difficulty in attracting staff as there were better opportunities elsewhere. Asylum-seeking refugees still managed to make it to Britain. Until they were processed, most were not allowed to work or claim benefit. Left with little choice, they entered the black economy instead, further depressing wages and adding to the crime rate.

The Coming of Donald Trump

When Donald Trump won the race to the White House in 2016 it unleashed a financial tsunami that quickly travelled around the globe. There were two main planks to Trump's manifesto that spooked the bond markets, huge borrowing to fund new public infra-structure and create jobs and protectionism. America was going to issue vast amounts of government bonds and this would both inflate the bond market, costing smaller coun-tries a packet and hit the value of the dollar which underpinned many other currencies. Danger loomed and the fear in economic circles became palpable. However, President Trump had yet another card up his sleeve, deregulating America's banks. Trump had long complained that American banks were strangled by red tape and wanted them freed up to take more risks, this was music to Wall Street ears and it quickly geared up to make hay. After Trump's victory was declared, shares in JP Morgan, Morgan Stanley and Citigroup had soared by more than 10%. The loosening of the fetters on America's banks quickly threatened what was left of Europe's banking sector. Before the financial crisis, Deutsche Bank, Credit Suisse and UBS were at the top of the global league tables. However by 2015 US banks dominated. Regulatory clampdowns and collapsing EU economies had knocked Europe's big investment banks for six. RBS had already given up trying to compete against Wall Street with UBS and Credit Suisse following suit. According to Richard Burton, CEO of UK equities at Old Mutual Global Investors *"Trump's presidency is hugely positive for US banks. They now have scope to expand and we are getting to a point where there won't be a big European investment bank."* Although the dollar soared under Trump, this acted against the President's plans to reduce imports and increase exports. Trump then had to talk down a by now volatile currency. The Americans were in for an interesting time on the Donald's helter-skelter. However, by making most of his appointments from outside the political elite, President Trump had changed the

15

nature of government and there would be no turning back. The new President took Ronald Reagan as his example and also put back the bust of Winston Churchill that had been removed by President Obama into the Oval Office. Two positive signs at least.

Britain: Spendthrift "Austerity"

Despite its grey cloak of austerity, Britain was now borrowing £3bn per week with almost half of it going directly to pay interest on the ever-increasing national debt. By this time, the awful reality was beginning to dawn that the government was incapable of controlling the spiralling debt crisis. Nevertheless, the Treasury continued to give assurances to bond markets while politicians showed no real understanding of the scale of the problem. Few had any experience of the real economy in any event. They had mostly been recruited straight from university as political researchers or been union officials without ever spending time on the shop floor.

An Excursus of Inflation

As paper currencies faltered, inflation grew and living standards fell still further. The press was full of the spectre of the Weimar Republic, where in 1923 hyperinflation took off. When their factories closed, workers had been paid off with currency that was inflating so rapidly that the printers gave up trying to print numbers on the bills. A loaf of bread that cost twenty thousand marks in the morning would cost five million marks by the evening. Those still in work had to be paid twice daily. Restaurant prices went up while customers were eating. The economy finally collapsed on 15 November when it took 4.2 trillion German marks to buy a single US dollar.

A more recent comparison was made with Argentina where, at the end of the twentieth century, government spending as a share of GDP had climbed to 30%. (In the UK in 2015, it was 44.4%.) Argentina had then been hit by a recession. Agricultural commodity prices slumped and, with the peso fixed by law at one-to-one with the US dollar, its exports were uncompetitive. The IMF stepped in on the assumption that, with restructuring, Argentina would bounce back with a growth rate of 3.5%. It managed only 0.5%.

Argentina had limited access to capital markets. Government bonds were sold short and the government found itself unable to borrow or meet debt payments. Meanwhile, pesos were converted into dollars and money fled the country. The government froze all bank accounts. Customers were only allowed to withdraw 250 pesos – later 300 – per week. No withdrawals were allowed from dollar accounts unless funds were first converted into pesos at a punitive rate of exchange.

By 2002 the Argentine economy had contracted by 20%. Output fell by more than 15%. Unemployment climbed over 25% and more than half the population found themselves living in poverty. The economy only began to recover when Argentina dropped the fixed exchange rate and there was a boom in commodity prices. Yet by spring 2016 Argentina was once again awash with cash as investors piled into what they now regarded as a safe haven.

The UK was not yet in such a precarious position. But, in 2013, Moody's had downgraded its AAA rating to AA1. By 2015, Standard & Poor still gave the UK an AAA negative rating, while Fitch gave it an AA+ stable. But with the government no longer handling the deficit effectively, Moody's, Standard & Poor's and Fitch's ratings slipped down into the Bs. The designation 'junk bond' was not far away. With its triple A rating long gone, interest rates on government bonds and coupons were forced sharply upwards. UK-based pension funds were also now investing overseas in direct contravention of legislation compelling them to buy mostly UK government bonds.

The cost of borrowing had increased from a low of 0.5% in 2010 and by May 2018 Britain faced paying 3% to attract funds. This represented a six-fold increase in real terms and the country was trapped in a lethal economic vortex with sterling being shorted in the market. To the man in the street nothing seemed particularly untoward but behind the scenes panic was setting in.

As Britain's credit rating slumped and interest rates on the national debt climbed, the government ordered the Bank of England to begin another programme of quantitative easing. This increased the amount of money in the economy, further fuelling inflation and pushing sterling ever closer to catastrophic devaluation. This is what happened to Zimbabwe in 2008 where the monthly inflation rocketed to 79.6bn% and prices were doubling every 24 hours. Barring Hungary this was the second-highest inflation rate ever recorded. In July 1946, the Hungarian pengö had a daily inflation rate of 207%, with prices doubling every fifteen hours. Pengö notes were overprinted in denominations of milpengö (One million pengö) and bilpengö (One million milpengö, one trillion pengö). The government stopped collecting taxes altogether as, by the time taxpayers paid up, it would be worthless.

In an attempt to stabilise the currency, the adópengö, or 'tax pengö' – an accounting unit used by the government and commercial banks – circulated alongside the pengö.

While even the 100m bilpengö note (100 *quintillion* pengö) was effectively worthless, the adópengö climbed to 2 x 1,021 pengö. On 1 August 1946, the pengö and adópengö were replaced by the forint at a rate of 400,000,000,000,000,000,000,000,000,000, 400 octillion or 4 x 1,029 pengö. The British were not quite yet sweeping up used notes from the street like the Hungarians but the omens were getting worse.

Zimbabwe's inflation had not been quite as bad, but a loaf of bread that cost Z$500 at the beginning of August in 2008 cost between Z$7,000 to Z$10,000 two months later. By then the official rate was Z$180 to the US dollar, though on the black market a US dollar fetched Z$8,000 – that is, for cash, which was in desperately short supply. For bank transfers, the rate was Z$1.5m to one. Those figures came after the currency was revalued in August, when ten zeros were knocked off. Plane loads of Zimbabwean dollars had to be flown in from the printers in Germany. In 2009, the government gave up printing its currency completely and adopted the US dollar, not that this made its people more affluent, just the chosen few.

Meanwhile the British managed to keep the lid on sterling – just. The IMF flew in, but they could only offer advice as their other member countries had similar problems and the entire Eurozone was itself now poised on a knife-edge.

Britain: The Downward Slide Continues

The International Monetary Fund had been set up at the end of World War II to stabilise exchange rates. In 2015 it had joined with Eurozone countries in helping to bail out Greece, provided that it continued its austerity policies.

Britain had been in a similar position at the end of 1975 when Labour's Chancellor of the Exchequer, Denis Healey, approached the IMF for help with the UK's balance of payments. The following year, he suffered public humiliation when he was forced to abandon his trip to a finance ministers' meeting in Hong Kong. He turned back at Heathrow Airport as intense nervousness hit the financial markets. From October to December the government held tense negotiations with the IMF, which demanded £2.5bn in cuts in government spending in return for a $3.9bn loan. There was no breathing space. That December, Healey had to produce a mini-budget implementing the cuts.

He later claimed that in hindsight the 1976 IMF loan had been unnecessary as the Treasury had grossly overestimated Britain's public sector borrowing requirement. Nevertheless, he called the loan a 'Pyrrhic defeat' because, by accepting the IMF terms, Britain had been forced into doing what it needed to do anyway.

Afterwards, Prime Minister James Callaghan told the Labour Party conference: 'We used to think that you could spend your way out of a recession and increase employment by cutting taxes and boosting government spending. I tell you in all candour that that option no longer exists, and insofar as it ever did exist, it only worked on each occasion since the war by injecting a bigger dose of inflation into the economy, followed by a higher level of unemployment as the next step.' Wise words indeed.

This was seen as the beginning of what became Thatcherite economics that attempted to rein in government spending from 1979 to 1997 – without notable success, as government spending as a share of GDP had continued to hover around 40%.

James Callaghan's words were not only accurate, they were prophetic and among the most important ever in British politics. A left-wing prime minister admitting that too much state spending was dangerous, 'whilst being barracked by a rabble of bearded Trotskyists from within his own party', marked a turning point in Western economic policymaking. For a time at least.

In 1976 the UK government had to go cap in hand to beg for an IMF bailout. After years of subsidising nationalised industries and soft budgets, Britain was insolvent. After months of denial, Callaghan's government had to face reality.

The Keynesian consensus then as now had been that the state could borrow and spend without limit to keep the economy afloat. However, Jim Callaghan's words blew this idea out of the water, albeit not for all that long.

In February 2010, in the run-up to a general election, twenty leading economists backed George Osborne's plan to cut the UK's annual fiscal shortfall over five years. However, some soon recanted and said that the Chancellor now should water down his plan and provide more 'fiscal stimulus'.

'Growth versus austerity' is a deliberately misleading phrase used for political point scoring by oppositions that do not need to accept any responsibility for government spending. Economic growth is not simply a matter of choice for a government, it is instead one of a number of possible outcomes resulting from whatever policies they follow.

It is of course much easier to inadvertently prevent growth from taking place. One red light that was about to shine bright was private investors refusing to buy any more government bonds: IOUs. That risked chaos in the markets sending interest rates through the roof. Once a country has printed too much money, its creditors realise that they will be repaid in a devalued currency and look elsewhere to invest. Unfortunately this had yet still to penetrate the usual thick skulls who insisted that, with borrowing rates so low, now was a good time for the government to spend heavily on infrastructure, whether it was needed or not. One example was HS2 which would have had few users at £500 for a London–Birmingham return. HS2 provided clear evidence of the lack of intellectual firepower now bedevilling the corridors of power. Lightweight politicians had somehow convinced themselves that faster trains could produce the same transformative effect that the arrival of steam-powered locomotives had delivered in the Victorian era. Policy by the rear-view mirror. Not only would the tickets have been prohibitively expensive but the only people able to afford them now used travelling time as working time with free Wi-Fi in most carriages and waiting rooms. Bought online, a single ticket for a 1hour 26minute London Birmingham train journey could be had for as little as £6.00.

Crowd-Funding the Way to Reform

By now, there was no way that any political party could have reversed this situation as even admitting to the true extent of our problems would have destroyed it. The only possible way to get reform underway would be for the electorate to continue the process started by Brexit and Trump to overturn the establishment. Campaigning groups began piling on pressure by crowd-funding independent candidates to challenge the big guys. They claimed that if MPs were to be selected by their constituents on their merits, rather than by party managers on their loyalty, matters could only improve. By now people were crying out for competent government by consensus rather than incompetent government by conflict. Coalition government had worked during WW2 so there was precedent for modifying our adversarial system. Simply keeping on doing the same thing whilst hoping for a different result was not going to work and would block the reforms needed. If political tribalism was not replaced by a system of government that was fit for purpose, and soon, the United Kingdom would not recover and might not even remain united.

By any analysis, political chicanery and tribalism lay at the heart of most of our problems. If political parties had to operate without the protection of parliamentary privilege they would have fallen foul of the Bribery Act, the Competition and Markets Authority, the Trades Description Act and Employment Law. Such was the damage that they had caused, that there was a growing case for banning them altogether. However, the shadowy form of a new political system was at last taking shape.

One of the most significant problems of such a febrile and antagonistic political atmosphere was the gulf between enterprise and government. Less so perhaps with the Conservative Party but as the Tories were forced onto the centre ground this changed. The long-promised bonfires of red tape never happened and enterprise came under increasing pressure on all fronts, not least with the imposition of the so-called 'living wage' which caused even more redundancies. Care homes that were already struggling with the Working Time Directive closed down, placing an even bigger burden on the NHS, and the black economy grew stronger still.

Private Enterprise: A Resource Untapped, but Heavily Milked

As well as providing almost all government revenue, the private sector delivered an extensive range of goods and services at affordable prices. However, instead of being relied on to resolve some of our most intractable problems, it was used as a cash cow and ignored. Mindful of their social responsibilities, many business people did try to provide assistance with local initiatives. Occasionally they succeeded but more often they were shunned by from narrow-minded politicians and bureaucrats protecting their own territory. As a result, little of the skill and experience generated within the business community was used for the greater good. Because of the nature of the political system pre the 2020s, business people kept well clear. However, once the tribalism started to disappear they quickly stepped up to the plate.

Such was the gap that had formed between government and enterprise that a vast industry of lobbyists and PR companies had sprung up in a futile, but highly lucrative, exercise to reconnect them. One way forward would be for those with managerial skills and resources to step up to the plate and help the electorate to overcome political stasis by rolling out exciting and innovative local projects. To change the way our country was governed we would first of all have to persuade the electorate that they had the power to achieve this. A group of entrepreneurs, including Richard Branson, offered £10,000 awards to the winners of competitions to find the best independent candidate in every Westminster constituency. This in turn stimulated crowd-funding and independent candidates were soon able to challenge the big guns and break their stranglehold.

Private Enterprise: Regulation by Consent

Another problem encountered by enterprise was their poor quality of representation. Employers had trade associations just as employees had trade unions. These associations were supposed to interact with the government and civil service to keep legislation as business friendly as possible. In theory, this allowed directors to concentrate on business, but their trust had been seriously misplaced.

Those with the sharpest elbows often get the best deals and some associations were noticeably more effective than others. A good example was farming, before the subsidies disappeared. Farmers were represented by the National Farmers Union, NFU, and had gained relief from business rates and planning restrictions whilst enjoying tax allowances, estate duties and subsidies along with rebated rates of fuel and road fund duty that other businesses could only dream about. So what did the NFU have that other associations lacked? For starters, most of its decision-makers were themselves active farmers and provided backbone to negotiations.

In contrast, the big trade associations were run by professionals, sometimes with an industry background but more often from politics or public relations. Their message might have been more sophisticated but their members had to contend with punitive rates of taxation, byzantine planning laws and gold-plated regulations. Major trade association get-togethers were top-down events. Instead of providing a venue for members to coalesce and act in concert, they had become soapboxes for their well-paid bosses. Close ties with senior politicians formed a significant part of their appeal and few conferences took place without the appearance of a member of government. However, more benefit accrued to the legislators than to fee-paying members.

The professionals who ran the large associations had to pay a heavy price for their access to the political machine. They dared not subject government to damning critiques, nor could they promote active dissent, as unions and farmers had often done with some success. No matter how poorly conceived or destructive new legislation might be, withering criticism or organised resistance would simply not take place. Governments were keen to maintain this arrangement which was the principal reason why ministers were willing participants at so many trade association conferences. Associations often claimed a result when all they had actually achieved was a short postponement. It soon became clear that a great deal of damaging legislation could have been avoided altogether if a meaningful effort had actually been made. However, major trade associations were controlled by major companies who were not only better equipped to deal with complex legislation; they regarded it as invaluable in suppressing SME competition.

The usual analysis of what the economists call "regulatory capture" describes how any regulatory agency created by the Government may come to view the world through the eyes of the industry it is supposed to control. However, with compliant trade associations, the opposite was more likely to occur as their lightweight leaders went out of their way to please the regulators.

Climate change legislation had been one of the more striking instances of this relationship. Despite mankind accounting for only two per cent of total CO_2 emissions (and the UK less than two per cent of that) a large number of hugely expensive initiatives had been spawned. Renewable Obligations and Carbon Charging ran side-by-side with subsidies for inefficient renewable energy schemes and inflated power bills. Trade associations sent out really mixed messages on this one. On the one hand they welcomed government initiatives to go green, the CBI even formed its very own climate change board, whilst on the other they warned of the dangers of increasing the cost of business energy and exporting jobs. Green initiatives had simply become revenue raisers, the environment often suffered and business was hit by increased regulation and higher costs. A number of studies concluded that, because of the enormous costs, for every job created in the green economy, at least three jobs were lost elsewhere. The CBI criticised the 50% reduction in feed-in tariffs for solar energy, as damaging to the nascent solar industry, yet the majority of their members were now suffering from inflated power bills. It also ignored the immorality of generous subsidies to those exploiting renewable energy subsidies to extract profit at a time of rising fuel poverty. A slightly warmer climate would have benefitted the UK but fuel poverty could be lethal.

Chapter Two – Freefall

The knock-on effects of Brexit were now working their way through the system and it was in one of the supposedly strongest countries, Germany, that the first really serious event took place. In a desperate attempt to stay solvent, two of its biggest banks, the Deutsche Bank and Commerzbank had merged. However, such was the toxic nature of their combined debt book that investors fled, taking what cash they could. After more than twenty-five years of buying up banks and overvalued assets around the world, the Deutsche Bank in particular had the capability to spark a crisis in the wider global economy. The IMF had called Deutsche 'the world's most dangerous bank', and briefed government officials that 'if Deutsche Bank goes down, everyone else has a problem too'.

The First Eurozone

Brexit had breached the dam and from then on the collapse of the Eurozone was just a matter of time. A similar monetary union had been tried in Europe once before. In 1865, France, Belgium, Italy and Switzerland formed the Latin Monetary Union, LMU. They agreed to produce gold and silver coins to the same standard. Greece joined in 1867. Spain and Romania did not formally join, but produced coins to LMU standards. Austria–Hungary also produced gold coins that were interchangeable. The French colonies of Algeria and Tunisia also found themselves in the LMU. Peru, Columbia and Venezuela accepted the franc. Serbia, Bulgaria and the Danish West Indies followed suit. And when Albania gained its independence from the Ottoman Empire in 1912, LMU coins circulated there.

By then, the LMU had already run into difficulties thanks to Greece. To prop up its weak economy, it began debasing the currency by decreasing the amount of gold in their coins. Greece was formally expelled from the LMU in 1908, but readmitted in 1910.

Others had also been playing fast and loose with the LMU. The Papal States began debasing the silver coins. Swiss and French banks rejected their coins and the Papal States were also ejected from the Union. In the meantime, the Papal Treasurer, Cardinal Giacomo Antonelli, had accumulated a considerable personal fortune. On his death, the Papal Treasury was found to be short of forty-five million lire.

The system became increasingly unstable as the supply of silver increased, making it overvalued in comparison with gold. Other problems arose when paper money was issued, backed by the LMU. World War I put an end to the LMU in practice and it was formally ended in 1927 due to the growing financial chaos.

America: The Impact of Donald Trump

While the Eurozone was crumbling, America was bucking the trend in style. When Donald Trump first became a serious contender for the presidency, the economists had made a long list of scary predictions that failed to materialise. However, the political pundits had also predicted a problem which looked equally plausible, a fiscal battle between the Republicans and Democrats. So far, there had been eighteen funding gaps in the US when Congress refused to pass a budget or the president vetoed it. The longest occurred in 1978, when the federal government was shut down for eighteen days after President Jimmy Carter vetoed a public works appropriations bill and a defence bill that included funding for a nuclear-powered aircraft carrier. Spending for the Department of Health, Education and Welfare was also delayed over disputes concerning Medicaid funding for abortion. The following year, the federal government was shut down again for a further eleven days – this time due to a dispute between the senate and the House of Representatives. Against the opposition of the senate, the House pushed for a 5.5% pay increase for members of Congress and senior civil servants. The House also sought to restrict federal spending on abortion only to cases where the mother's life was in danger, while the senate wanted to maintain funding for abortions in cases of rape and incest.

Democrat President Bill Clinton locked horns with a Republican Congress over the budget for twenty-one days over Christmas and New Year in 1995–6, but essential government work continued until a compromise was reached. A Republican House tried to shut down the government again in 2013 in an attempt to force the Democrats to delay President Barack Obama's signature on healthcare reforms. All non-essential government services were stopped for sixteen days.

Although few had predicted Donald Trump beating Hilary Clinton to become the forty-fifth American president, no one had imagined that the Republicans would also take control of the Senate and the House of Representatives. The political scenario in the US immediately became highly polarised even before President elect Trump took office. Distraught and furious Democrat supporters took to the streets and called for Trump to be impeached for corporate fraud and sexual harassment. This of course infuriated Trump's supporters and for a while it looked like America could be heading for another civil war. Trump wanted to close down all imports from 'unfriendly' countries, such as China and give US companies with branches overseas an ultimatum: they could either repatriate their head offices and profit to America or they would be banished from the US market. Business was appalled but the blue-collar workers and rednecks who had elected Trump were cock-a-hoop.

The US administration's unfettered insularism and fiscal easing was a significant short term success for America but destabilised the dollar. China held massive foreign exchange reserves, most of it in dollars. Tensions over Taiwan and the Senkaku islands, claimed by China but held by Japan in the East China Sea, and fresh sabre rattling between North and South Korea – client states of China and the US respectively – would give Beijing a powerful incentive to wipe out the American economy by flooding the world markets with greenbacks. The tidal wave of collapse would spread around the same way as it had after the Wall Street Crash of 1929, causing the ten-year Great Depression that affected all Western industrialised countries. This resulted in mass unemployment and the rise of Nazism with the world economy only reviving with the onset of World War II.

Britain: Austerity with a Lash

It was clear that the world was on the edge of the abyss, and in June 2018 the UK Chancellor delivered an emergency budget unlike any that had gone before. All public sector salaries and pensions were cut by 30% with immediate effect; likewise 30% of personal cash balances over £75,000 and business reserves over 10% of gross annual profit were transferred to the Treasury and government bonds issued in their place.

These measures were much more drastic than the cuts that felled Ireland, the Celtic Tiger, following the banking collapse. After years of high growth, the Irish GDP had suddenly contracted by 14% during 2008. Successive budgets slashed €18.5bn from public spending while raising another €12bn in taxes. Some 37,500 public service staff were laid off, a ten per cent cut. Spending on health services was cut by 27%. Capital expenditure on important public infrastructure was reduced by 60% between 2008 and 2014, while €17bn of the national pension reserve was put into the bailout.

By 2015, 37,000 Irish homeowners were in mortgage arrears of over 720 days and legal repossession notices were issued to 50,000 households. Debt interest payments rose from €2bn, or 3.4% of tax revenue, in 2007, to a staggering €7.5bn, or 18% of all tax revenue in 2014. Charges were introduced on water, property, school transport, prescriptions, A&E and chemotherapy. These had all been free before.

Ireland's child poverty rose from 18% in 2008 to 29.1% in 2013. The rate of deprivation increased from 26.9% in 2012 to 30.5% in 2013 while for lone-parent families it had risen to 63%. Food poverty affected 600,000, a climb of 13.2%. During the boom years, émigrés had begun returning to Ireland, but during the recession almost 10% of young people left. Otherwise the unemployment rate would have risen to 20%. In the wake of the 2008 banking crisis, the UK offered to help Ireland out. This time it was Britain that needed help.

Despite the UK's well-oiled government spin machine insisting that the Treasury's current strictures were a one-off event, there was an immediate run on sterling and credit cards became useless, as traders demanded cash instead. People were shocked to find that, not only was the austerity programme not working, but they had been kept in the dark about the full extent of the problem. For ten solid years the country had suffered 'death by a thousand cuts' but all for nothing. In America President Trump nodded sagely having long predicted that the European model was headed for a brick wall. This however gave him two further reasons not to bail out America's overseas allies. Firstly he reckoned that they needed a hard lesson to teach them the profligate error of their ways. However, more importantly, as a long term entrepreneur, Donald Trump recognised and respected the force of creative destruction. More than most, he realised that Europe needed a fresh start and the only way to achieve this would be to destroy the *status quo* and rebuild from the ground up.

Lessons from the Past: Gold Standard to Exchange Rate Mechanism

Politicians will often stick to a doomed policy rather than abandon it and admit they were wrong; this is precisely what happened during the ERM fiasco of 1992. The European Exchange Rate Mechanism had been set up in 1979. The idea was to stabilise the exchange rates between European currencies prior to the introduction of the euro in 1999. Britain did not join. However, by 1987 the Treasury was following a semi-official policy of shadowing the West German Deutschmark. This resulted in a clash between the Chancellor of the Exchequer Nigel Lawson and Prime Minister Margaret Thatcher's economic advisor Alan Walters, who considered the ERM 'half-baked'. Both Lawson and Walters were forced to resign.

John Major took over as Chancellor and persuaded the government to sign up to the ERM. This committed Britain to following economic and monetary policies that would prevent the pound fluctuating more than 6% from other currencies. However, with interest rates at 15% and inflation running three times that of Germany, it was not a good time to join. What's more, after the fall of the Berlin Wall in 1989, German reunification proved costly when the East German Ostmark was exchanged one for one with the Deutschmark. The measures taken by the Bundesbank, to counteract the inflation that this caused, put a significant stress on the whole of the ERM.

Further instability was caused when the Danish electorate rejected the Maastricht Treaty, turning the European Community into the European Union and setting the stage for the introduction of the euro. It was then announced that there would be a referendum in France as well. A referendum on the Maastricht Treaty was duly held in France on 20 September 1992. It was approved by only 51% of the voters. The result of the referendum, known as the 'petit oui', along with the Danish 'No' vote signalled the end of the consensus on European integration which from then on was subject to much greater scrutiny.

Hungarian-born American investor George Soros spotted that Britain had joined the ERM at too high a rate. As the pound sank near the bottom of its band, the British government would be forced to prop it up – or leave the ERM. It was a matter of national prestige. On Tuesday 15 September 1992 Soros began selling pounds which, under the ERM regulations, the Bank of England was forced to buy.

When the markets opened on what became 'Black Wednesday', the Bank began buying orders of some £300m before 8.30 am. As the day went on, Soros continued to sell and the Bank of England continued to buy. John Major was then prime minister. His Chancellor, Norman Lamont told him that buying pounds was not having the desired effect of holding sterling within its ERM band.

In a desperate effort to hold the line, Lamont began increasing interest rates. During the day, base rate climbed from ten to 15%, a staggering 50% increase. But by 7 p.m., the game was up. The pound dropped out of the ERM and interest rates dropped back to 10%. The day's trading had cost Treasury £3.3bn.

Seeing such financial incompetence, public fury erupted. The inevitable protest marches and demonstrations quickly led to a general strike. There had, of course, been a general strike in Britain before. Although that had been a relatively good-natured affair, the causes were clear. In the years following World War I, coal mining in the UK found itself the doldrums. The price of coal on the international market had fallen due to increased competition from the US, Poland and Germany, which was exporting coal to France and Italy as part of its war reparations. Meanwhile, UK production slumped and miners were forced to take a pay cut.

In 1925, Winston Churchill, then Chancellor of the Exchequer, put the pound back on the gold standard. The strong pound further hurt exports. The mine owners announced another cut in wages and put an extra hour on the working day. If they would not accept these terms, the miners were threatened with a lockout, but they stood firm under the slogan: 'Not a penny off the pay, not a minute on the day'.

They had also formed an alliance with the railwaymen and other transport workers, who threatened to embargo any movement of coal. As coal was then the main source of heat and energy, this would have brought the country to a halt.

The Conservative government stepped in to provide a subsidy to mine owners which would avoid a pay cut for the miners. But the agreement only ran for nine months. Meanwhile they recruited a task force of volunteers to take over public transport in the event of a strike.

When the subsidy came to an end, the mine owners again insisted that they would have to cut pay and lengthen the working day. The Miners' Federation of Great Britain – the forerunner of the National Union of Mine Workers which was established in 1945 – refused to comply. When negotiations failed, the Trades Union Congress announced a general strike in support of the miners, beginning on 4th May 1926.

The following day, the country was at a standstill. But two days later, volunteers were manning the buses and Britain was on the move again. By the seventh day, the TUC came up with a set of proposals to end the strike, though they did not enjoy the support of the Miners' Federation. On the eighth day, the army broke through a picket line at the London docks to ensure food supplies. But the Prime Minister Stanley Baldwin took the precaution of not arming the soldiers, against the advice of Churchill.

On the tenth day, the TUC went to Downing Street and announced that they would call off the strike, though the miners remained out for a few more months. However, the general strike had passed off remarkably peacefully; successfully crushing the aspirations of many would-be revolutionaries in the process.

But times had changed. In the 'Winter of Discontent' of 1978–9, a series of strikes, overtime bans and other industrial action in pursuit of pay claims shut down various sections of industry. An unofficial strike of lorry drivers closed down petrol stations. The ports were picketed and over a million workers were laid off.

The government threatened to declare a state of emergency and the army were put on standby to take over from tanker drivers. However, the Transport and General Workers Union accepted that certain emergency supplies were exempted from action, but what should go on this list would be determined by local officials. When strikers in Hull did not allow various types of animal feed through to local farms, the farmers dropped the bodies of dead chickens and piglets outside the union's office. The union contended that the farmer had actually wrung the chicken's necks and the piglets had been killed when the sow rolled over and crushed them.

When some strikers won substantial pay rises, the strikes spread. Rail workers began a series of one-day strikes. Public sector unions held a 'Day of Action' but the army was brought in when ambulance drivers went on strike. Ancillary hospital staff also came out. NHS hospitals were only treating emergencies, with union officials scandalously deciding who got treatment and who did not.

Gravediggers went on strike and Liverpool City Council had to hire a factory to store corpses until they could be buried. The refuse collectors joined in, causing rubbish to be piled up in public parks, attracting rats to Leicester Square in the heart of London's West End.

At the height of the disruption, Prime Minister James Callaghan was famously interviewed at Heathrow Airport, having just returned from a summit in Guadeloupe where, he admitted to have taken a dip in the Caribbean.

Asked, 'What is your general approach, in view of the mounting chaos in the country at the moment?' Callaghan replied: 'Well, that's a judgment that you are making. I promise you that if you look at it from outside, and perhaps you're taking rather a parochial view at the moment, I don't think that other people in the world would share the view that there is mounting chaos.'

The next day's Sun carried the famous headline: '*Crisis? What crisis?*' – making Callaghan seem completely out of touch. An editorial in the Sun also borrowed the phrase 'Winter of Discontent' from Shakespeare's Richard III to describe the situation. This led to a landslide victory for the Conservative Party, headed by Margaret Thatcher, who promised to curb the unions and took on the NUM with resulting violence. Her term in office also witnessed the poll tax riots. Austerity-bound Britain also erupted with riots again in 2011, this time coordinated using Blackberries, mobile phones and social media. Approaching the end of the second decade of the twenty-first century, the stage was set for things to get much worse.

Crisis: The Confiscation of Cash

Britain was not the only country to suffer. The cost of borrowing across the whole of the Western world soared and currencies previously thought to be stable became vulnerable. The UK cash confiscation was the final straw and a wave of panic trashed the euro, sterling and dollar in quick succession. Paper currencies were referred to as fiat or faith currencies. They held no intrinsic value and once faith in them had evaporated, they quickly became worthless.

Such confiscations had taken place before, notably in the US in 1933. During the Great Depression the Federal Reserve came close to the limit it could borrow as this had to be backed by its holdings of gold under the Federal Reserve Act of 1913. Consequently, President Franklin D Roosevelt's government used wartime provisions to issue a presidential proclamation forbidding the hoarding of 'gold or silver or bullion or currency'. This was followed by an executive order that required everyone to surrender their gold – except for small amounts in the form of jewellery, historic coins or artefacts – to the federal government. In exchange, they were given dollar bills. The dollar was still on the gold standard, so a dollar bill could theoretically be redeemed as a dollar's-worth of gold. But as citizens were not allowed to own gold, this was worthless. This gave the Federal Reserve a free hand to issue as much credit as it liked, or thought it could get away with, by the simple expedient of devaluing the dollar, which it promptly did by 40%.

In 1959 the Australian government also passed a Banking Act that allowed it to seize private citizens' gold in return for paper money. Again in 2013, desperate to close a $13m deal with international bankers to prevent its financial collapse, the Cypriot government seized up to 40% of the assets of depositors who had more than €100,000 in the bank, including a number of Russian oligarchs who had thought their money would be safe there. The deal went ahead with the approval of other EU countries. This set a precedent that would prevent legal challenges to other governments seizing money held in a nation's banks.

Money printing had by now reached its inevitable conclusion and Western economies imploded with gold tripling in value overnight. In time-honoured fashion, governments had remained in denial until the bitter end and the first indication of the true scale of the disaster was troops on the streets with food and fuel being rationed.

The consequences of such financial recklessness have long been known. In 1694, Scottish Banker John Law was convicted of murder at the Old Bailey for killing an adversary in a duel in Bloomsbury Square and sentenced to hang. When this was commuted, he fled to Amsterdam. He returned to Scotland to take part in the debates in the run-up to the Treaty of Union in 1707. But when his proposal of establishing a national bank in Scotland was rejected he went back to the Continent.

At the beginning of the eighteenth century, the French government was heavily in debt as a result of the extensive wars of Louis XIV who died in 1715. Law proposed a public note-issuing bank, but the proposal was dismissed. A second proposal for a purely private bank was accepted in 1716, and the bank was licensed to issue notes for a twenty-year period. With little to restrain him, Law kept pumping out money. The huge expansion in the money supply eventually resulted in the collapse of the French economy. Evdenso, Law's bank, later became the Banque Royale, the French central bank.

Crisis: The Continuing Mountain of Debt

Not only had successive governments bribed the electorate with their own money, they were now bribing them with their children's money as well. We were imposing an enormous burden on future generations. Every baby born in the UK was already £24,000 in debt. By the time they were sixteen, this debt would have more than doubled. Those who found work would face a punitive level of lifelong taxation; those who couldn't would suffer an ever-decreasing level of public support. It had been known for parents to cut up an offspring's credit card but before long children would wish that they had cut up their parents' cards instead.

In October 2016 the International Monetary Fund warned that global debt had hit a record high of $152trillion but to the average man in the street this figure was meaningless. Few now bothered if the headlines involved millions, billions or trillions, it never seemed to be all that important. Printing money was now the norm; everyone was doing it so everything must be ok was the received wisdom of the day.

The warning came after the IMF cut its growth forecasts for a series of countries around the world, leaving Britain the fastest growing economy in the G7 – despite its recent Brexit vote. World debt was now two and a quarter times world GDP. This was a record high and had overtaken the reduction in borrowing caused by the 2008 crisis.

The economists went on to warn that the sheer scale of our debt was weighing down economic growth to such an extent that any fragile recovery could easily turn into stagnation or even recession. The economists were also worried that the populist policies of protectionism, now being put into motion in the US by President Trump and threatened throughout Europe by extremist right-wing politicians such as Marine Le Pen, would kick globalisation into reverse. This would immediately cripple international trade, investment and migration, sending the world economy into a prolonged period of stagnation or even a death spiral.

Warning of the effects of protectionism, the IMF said, 'These initiatives limit or reverse international trade and financial integration, generating a sell-off in stock markets on profitability concerns and reduced risk appetite, with the real equity price falling by 20% in the Eurozone, the UK and the US over two years. Banks could be crushed by the economic slump while private consumption and business investment would also fall, hitting growth further.'

In its carefully worded statement the IMF concluded, 'A combination of low growth, high debt and weak banks could push the world in a dangerous financial and political direction.' At least they got that one right.

The world did not rack up $152trillion of debt overnight; it was the combination of a borrowing binge in the years before the financial crisis, followed by policies such as quantitative easing. A desperate measure that could only be used so often.

Western economies had borrowed heavily in the boom years. In the UK and the US, governments stepped in to bail out banks, meaning the financial sector recovered – but governments ended up with huge debts. The Eurozone tried a slightly different route. This may have left some governments with less debt, but many of its banks were by now in very deep trouble indeed including the mighty German Deutsche Bank and Commerzbank.

In recent times government debt had become endemic with practically no chance of being repaid. Governments rarely now managed budget surpluses and continued to add to their borrowing year on year.

This did not actually have to be a major problem so long as the economy was also growing quickly. Unfortunately, by this time the world economy was contracting instead and some of the most indebted economies in the Western world were already very weak.

Just as a household runs into trouble when it has big debts but a flat or falling income, so governments struggle when GDP is flat. Over time interest payments mount up, adding to the debt even when the economy is not growing.

The IMF Steps In – and Out

Officials at the IMF believed that there were two ways to get out of this trap, although neither was painless. Central banks could slash interest rates to record lows, helping governments because their borrowing costs are very low and giving the indebted a little bit of breathing space. The officials also recommended that governments that could afford to spend more should do so, help banks clean up their bad loans and force inefficient companies to merge and cut costs. Governments with good banks could spend more on infrastructure to create jobs and boost the long-term potential of the economy.

The IMF also warned governments to get rid of the red tape that was strangling their economies. This would free up the over-regulated jobs markets, slash barriers to international trade and encourage research and development to boost productivity.

Governments had of course been trying to do this for years but had backed off in the face of stiff resistance from vested interests and opposition parties looking to score points. If the IMF's fears came true and governments moved in the opposite direction, closing borders and clamping down on trade, then a gloomy future of permanent debt and economic disappointment lay ahead. The IMF was seldom right in its predictions, or so its critics claimed, and its warnings fell on deaf ears. Early in the morning of 9 October 2016, sterling suddenly plummeted 6% in the Asian market. This was passed off as an electronic glitch referred to as a 'flash crash'. However, before long a 6% fall would look like very small beer indeed.

Chapter Three – Full Spectrum Crisis

In crisis-struck Britain, the supply of electricity rapidly became a major issue. Most of Britain's coal-fired power stations had been shut down by EU directives and replaced by gas and biofuel-fired plants as well as wind farms. However, Britain could no longer pay for imported gas or wood pellets, any local biofuel had long since been exhausted and our wind turbines produced only on an intermittent basis. From the beginning, the promise of renewable energy had been a pipe dream. The green lobby had found it easy to ride the tidal wave of environmentalism that had swept across Europe convincing gullible civil servants and lightweight politicians that their expensive toys actually worked. Not only could they get something for nothing but the votes would flood in as well, a win-win scenario. All you had to do, they said, was harness the limitless power of 'renewable energy' but there was no such thing as a free lunch.

There is no Such Thing as "Renewable Energy"

Fools often think that they can get something for nothing. Unfortunately a large number of our politicians agreed and decided to make their fantasy come true with public money. They thought all that was required was to harness the infinite power of wind, water and plant life. A concept so simple you have to wonder why it had not been done before. But of course it had and many centuries ago at that. The first recognisable windmill was produced two thousand years ago by a Greek known as Heron the Engineer; water power is even more ancient and goes back to the sixth millennium BC and the first patent for wave power was filed by a father-and-son team in Paris in 1799. The history of tidal power goes back as far as 900 AD.

Wind power was used successfully to pump small amounts of water and charge DC batteries where mains electricity was not an option. Hydropower produced about 18%

of the world's electricity and 95% of all the 'renewable' energy claimed was actually from hydro or biofuel. Wave power remained a pipe dream despite thousands of patents, hundreds of prototypes and many millions handed out in research grants. Tidal power was most effectively captured by a barrage but the large Le Rance tidal power station near St Malo could only supply a mere 0.012% of France's electricity.

The first problem with so-called wind turbines was that these machines were not actually turbines at all, the term had been corrupted. Turbines traditionally worked with contained flows at high pressure. Wind 'turbines' were actually rotors or variable pitch propellers in open flow. According to Betz' law they were at best only 59% efficient in kinetic terms as almost half of the wind leaks to the periphery, bypassing the blades altogether. They also only record around 30% productivity due to variable wind speeds, giving an overall approximate efficiency of 18%. Massive machines, huge costs but only a pitiful return. There were even more drawbacks; due to their complexity and the huge stresses involved, they only had a twenty to twenty-five-year maximum lifespan. They were also hugely problematic to keep operational, especially offshore. Not only were they dependent on ongoing subsidy to operate, once that subsidy was withdrawn, they could not be replaced. Some 14,000 abandoned wind turbines already littered America, with Spain and Portugal not far behind. The sheer volume of birds and bats killed by their spinning blades, with tip speeds approaching 400 mph had also been kept from public scrutiny. An enormous number of landowners, speculators and consultants were on this gravy train and inconvenient facts, such as bird kills, were kept under wraps.

Bio-fuel was another big mistake. Not only did burning wood pellets produce more greenhouse gasses per Kilowatt produced but we had to import them. The wood pellet industry claimed that the pellets were manufactured from bark and off-cuts but with some eight million tonnes being imported every year by the UK alone this simply wasn't possible. The theory that every tree felled would be replaced did not stand scrutiny. Replacing mature trees weighing many tonnes with seedlings was totally ineffectual. An English power station, Drax, was the biggest biomass generator in the world. In 2015, it burned more timber than the UK produced in total. At its peak it was getting £1.5m per day in subsidies to burn wood being shipped all the way from Canada. All that to produce less than one percent of the UK's electricity requirement. Growing corn for bio-fuel in countries like Brazil, drove up the cost of basic food so much that riots were caused.

There are two types of freshwater hydropower, single pass and pumped storage. Single pass systems are a successful, predictable and low-cost option but totally dependent on rainfall over an enormous catchment area and the best sites had already been utilised.

However that didn't stop the speculators installing single pass systems and many rivers now had dry stretches with their water in a pipe. Small hydro schemes were given even bigger subsidies than other forms of renewables and the gravy train quickly appeared. Pumped storage systems, using a header reservoir, were originally designed to soak up 'free' nuclear-generated electricity at night-time and return it intermittently throughout the next day to back up thermal and nuclear generation at times of peak demand. A first class concept but not one that could be used to replace base load thermal generation.

Some 30% of power is lost due to pumping inefficiencies and pipe friction. However, more problematical is their limited capacity. The UK's largest pumped storage power stations, Dinorwig in Wales and Cruachan in the Scottish Highlands can only hold a maximum of ten hours' supply at peak load and are net users of electricity. Pumped storage reservoirs also have a major ecological impact by flooding large areas.

If ever there was a fantasy then it surely was wave power. Despite increasingly desperate efforts by engineers and politicians alike, a viable machine had never been built. The Scottish government in particular wasted in excess of £30m of taxpayers' money subsidising madcap schemes such as the Salter Duck, the Sea Oyster and the Pelamis Sea Snake. The most impressive component of these machines was the sheer quality of their paintwork. This gave them the 'wow factor' required to convince unqualified civil servants and other potential funders of their worth. Even after Pelamis went into liquidation, the Scottish government shelled out yet more money for its worthless patents. They also announced additional multimillion-pound research funding but their £10m Saltire wave power prize was never claimed. Eventually the penny dropped and spendthrift politicians once again found out that even unlimited funding could not overcome the laws of physics. Sometimes these darn pigs just refuse to get airborne no matter what you do.

Estuary barriers such as Le Rance do work although their overall efficiency is low due to the four periods of slack water every day. The environmental disturbance is significant, the capital costs are high and construction takes at least ten years. Plans for a tidal barrage across the Severn Estuary were two hundred years old but had never been progressed.

Large tidal propellers had also been installed in areas with faster-than-normal tides such as Strangford Lough and the Sound of Islay. Plans and funding had also been approved for a large number of seabed tidal generators in the Pentland Firth; the Meygen project. By this time, the authorities had become wary and Meygen was initially limited to five units to prove their capability. However, even though water was a much more powerful medium than air, the enormous sums required to achieve pitifully small and intermittent returns proved insurmountable and this project was also abandoned.

Due to its northerly, rain soaked, location and topography, Norway had an enormous surplus of hydro-electricity which it offered to the British government, by way of an interconnector, at only £40/MW. In comparison, the planned new French–Chinese nuclear power station at Hinkley Point had been given a guarantee of £92.50/MW and for thirty years. The levelised cost of onshore wind was £150/MW with offshore almost double that. So-called renewable energy systems could never have replaced nuclear or gas-fired generation in any event because of three basic and insurmountable problems. They were all intermittent and, in the case of wind, unpredictable as well. In addition they all depended on locally weak, dispersed sources of energy using very expensive, complex machinery, but the killer blow was the inability to store significant amounts of high voltage electricity. Not that this hadn't been attempted with a number of prototypes having been trialled. These included compressed gas reservoirs and massive steel spinning wheels referred to as Flywheel Energy Storage, neither of which could be up-scaled sufficiently to meet demand. A great deal of time and money was also invested in making batteries more efficient, but once again these were only suitable for small-scale applications such as household lighting. Electric vehicles were a success for city travel but required a 24/7 means of recharging. Although the notion of clean, carbon-free power from infinite sources had obvious appeal, in reality it could not happen without an unaffordable amount of consumer subsidy. In one highly amusing episode, an official Chinese delegation led by Vice Premier Mr Li visited the Pelamis factory in Edinburgh. His 'security staff' spent several days beforehand making sure all would be safe for the visit. Some days after Mr Li's party departed, the Pelamis offices were broken into and some design laptops stolen. Needless to say an exact replica duly appeared in China, albeit with rather less attractive paintwork. It was no longer referred to as a sea snake; it was now named the Sea Dragon. However, even the Chinese couldn't get it to work and it disappeared never to be seen again.

Conventional sources of electricity were surcharged by Green levies to make the highly inefficient renewables sector seem more attractive. Despite a belated attempt to give relief to energy-intensive industries by way of a rebate, it was too little too late. The damage had been done and many of the UK's heavy industries were now based overseas where power was much cheaper. Favoured countries included America where shale gas and oil had slashed energy prices.

The renewable energy episode had turned out to be a hugely expensive mistake with landscapes blighted and businesses ruined in the process. However, it taught us that we needed people in government with sufficient real-world experience to see through extravagant claims made by sharp-suited salesmen bearing glossy brochures.

As Britain found itself running out of power, some elderly nuclear plants had been given a last-minute reprieve but insufficient capacity remained and the national grid failed. The tiny and intermittent amounts from renewable sources were useless without base load capacity and the lights went out. However, water and sewage was a much bigger problem than lighting. Water supplies failed and sewage pipes backed up as their pumps fell silent.

Britain: A Slide into State Socialism

The government soon discovered that it was out of its depth. In an attempt to prevent a slide into anarchy, it adopted a wartime stance and installed a command economy in the private sector to 'maximise output'. The harsh lessons of post-war nationalisation had been forgotten. In the heady days following the Second World War, nationalisation became a fundamental part of the Labour Party programme of 'creating a country fit for heroes'. The state took control of a wide range of assets and industries. Shipbuilding, steel, coal, docks along with air, sea, road and rail travel were commandeered 'for the greater good'. The state seized car, bus, truck and tractor factories as well with even Thomas Cook & Son the travel agent being nationalised in a veritable blitzkrieg of compulsory purchase. Despite stiff resistance from the British Medical Association, Britain's health service was also nationalised in July 1948 to become the NHS. Clement Attlee later admitted that he had overcome the objections of doctors by 'stuffing their mouths with gold'. Little wonder perhaps that doctors remained the staunchest defenders of the NHS as well as its biggest critics. All the nationalised enterprises rapidly developed similar problems. The combination of political point scoring, weak management, restrictive practices and militant unions eventually forced their repatriation to the private sector. Most of the enterprises once privatised recovered and some, such as British Airways, went on to become world class.

Needless to say the latest command economy was also a disaster. Department heads would report their output to the factory boss who, in turn, would report to the regional planner. The regional planner would then send a report to the central state planning authority, who would then make decisions which were passed back down the chain of command.

No one wanted to admit failure, so everyone lied and exaggerated. Factory managers would claim that they had met, or exceeded, targets even though output was slumping. As the state sought to maintain the illusion of full employment, bosses were given an incentive to take on people at no extra cost. The more people under their control, the more important they seemed. Bureaucrats indulged in empire building while productivity nosedived. The politicians had ended up making matters even worse for all concerned. By now the population was far removed from its comfort zone and the mood turned nasty. Widespread civil disorder kicked off with looters raiding shops and businesses. Immigrants and ethnic minorities were also targeted and sought protection in fortified enclaves. Politicians and administrators followed suit and many were forced to travel with armed guards or go into hiding. Public offices closed down, banks were vandalised and large numbers of the police and armed forces stayed home to protect their own families as best they could. Panic and violence ruled the streets whilst the rest of the world looked on in helpless amazement. Being nationwide, the problem was beyond a conventional response as the first responders were themselves out of action. Some emergency planning did come good and special units of the army manned broadcasting stations and began transmitting appeals for calm. Food stores released what supplies they had and some essential services resumed using standby generators. A number of countries started to mobilise aid but by then the situation was desperate. Food alone could not prevent anarchy nor reason overcome panic. Adding to the mayhem were Russian-funded agitators calling for the government to be overthrown.

The Voluntary Sector Rises to the Challenge

Just when it looked as if matters were going to get completely out of hand, the mood changed yet again. Once people realised that the regular services were not going to be able to take control of the situation, their survival instincts kicked in. Natural leaders began to exert control and localised pockets of order formed. Fortunately it was by now summer and hypothermia was not a threat. The first priority was food; power failures had wiped out virtually all frozen supplies leaving only limited quantities of tinned and dry goods. Farmers could no longer step into the breach as many of them had switched to biofuel and timber to collect green subsidies. Little grain was left after a long winter and no fresh crops were due before late summer. However, helped by the army, most dairy, pig and poultry farmers managed to obtain generators and sufficient fuel to restart production. Temporary abattoirs were set up and basic supply lines reinstated. Some food and fuel also began to arrive from overseas often courtesy of Norway or one of the Commonwealth countries.

As both capitalism and socialism had palpably failed, other models were tried. One of the more successful was the 'gift economy'. During earlier economic downturns people had bartered, swapping fixing someone's car for a few hours' babysitting. In parts of the Pacific and among some of the Indian tribes on the West Coast of America, entire economies exist on giving. People give to others knowing that others will do the same for them. Giving without expectation of getting anything in return is thought to be poisonous, as if the donor was passing on their sins with the gift. The gift economy carried its own incentives, and they were powerful. People who gave the most gained social status, while those who took without giving very soon changed their ways and became contributors in whatever way they could.

These cooperative ideas were not new to Britain. Chocolate-maker George Cadbury built the village of Bourneville for his workers to improve their living conditions. Earlier mill-owner Robert Owen, recognised founder of the cooperative movement, had done the same for his workers in New Lanark. Owen opened the first school for infants in Great Britain at New Lanark along with a not-for-profit co-op shop for his workers. The village became a UNESCO world heritage centre and a place of global pilgrimage for social reformers.

Impatient with the speed of social reform in the UK, Owen bought 30,000 acres of land in Indiana and established New Harmony there. After two years, the experiment failed with Owen having lost 80% of his fortune. Back in Britain, he tried again at Queenwood in Hampshire. Disciples set up other Owenite communities at Orbiston near Glasgow and Ralahine, County Cork. He continued teaching his communitarian principles. His son, who grew up in New Lanark and edited the *New Harmony Gazette*, set up a new community at Nashoba, Tennessee, dedicated to the education and emancipation of slaves. As a congressman he introduced the bill that created the Smithsonian Institution and at the outbreak of the Civil War he lobbied President Lincoln to end slavery.

America had produced many philanthropists. One was George Peabody who, on a business trip to England, negotiated an $8m loan for the near-bankrupt state of Maryland, taking no commission on the transaction. He provided Baltimore with a library, art gallery and music academy and funded a museum of archaeology at Harvard, a natural history museum at Yale and a historical museum and library in his hometown of South Danvers, Massachusetts, which later changed its name to Peabody. He gave $3.5m to the Peabody Education Trust to promote the education of southern children of all races and another $2.5m for the construction of apartments for London's working people. This was the origin of the Peabody Trust and many wealthy British people were to follow suit. Perhaps they were mindful of the following passage from the bible, '*It is easier for a camel to go through the eye of a needle, than for a rich man to enter into the kingdom of God.*' But more likely would have been a desire to earn the respect of their peers.

In the new-style economy, country dwellers had an advantage over those in towns and cities where not only was food and fuel a problem, most services had also ground to a halt. Water supplies were at best intermittent, bins were not emptied and the stench of untreated sewage permeated the streets. However, after the initial disturbances, crime levels had fallen. Even criminals had families to look after and feared the instant justice being meted out by irate citizens.

People naturally pull together after a disaster. After Hurricane Katrina hit New Orleans, there was some looting of stores, but largely because survivors were short of food. There were also reports of carjacking, murders, thefts and rapes, but it was later discovered that many of the reports were inaccurate, greatly exaggerated or completely false and the news agencies had to issue retractions.

It was also said that many of the refugees from the disaster had criminal records and caused a crime wave in the surrounding states that took them in. Of the 350 refugees who fetched up in West Virginia, 45% had criminal records and 22% had convictions for violent crimes. However, a study of the crime statistics showed no increase in the states that took evacuees.

Precedents for Spontaneous Order

And order can emerge from chaos. For many years in Mexico, the drug cartels operated almost unchecked. Corruption in high places made it impossible for government to crack down on them. However, citizens began to take things into their own hands. In the mountains of Guerrero, the *Auto Defensa* movement sprang up. This was an autonomous uprising of *compesinos* who had been pushed too far by the gangsters and were determined to regain control of their towns and villages. On 5 January 2013, in Ayutla de los Libres, a town of around 30,000 people, the local *comisario*, or police chief, was kidnapped. The residents armed themselves and closed the roads in and out of town. Patrols soon found the *comisario* and freed him. His captors were taken prisoner instead.

This was not technically a vigilante action. Under the Mexican constitution, indigenous communities in some parts of the country were allowed to form their own police force. So the locals kicked out both the municipal and federal police. Donning masks and wielding shotguns and machetes, they began clearing the streets of criminals and crime was quickly reduced by 90%.

Guerrero's Governor Ángel Heladio Aguirre Rivero praised their efforts. But some were critical of what had become the *Policia Communitaria*, or community police force, saying that they violated human rights by denying those accused due legal process. Around sixty prisoners held in a makeshift prison were paraded in front to crowds to shame them. The stout resistance of the residents of Ayutla de los Libres inspired other towns and villages in Guerrero to take up arms against the cartels.

Low-tech solutions were deployed while sophisticated machinery lay idle; bicycles and wind-up radios were in particular demand. People began to look back to the ideas of British economist E.F. Schumacher who published *Small is Beautiful: A Study of Economics As If People Matter* during the 1973 energy crisis and emergence of globalisation. In it, he argued that the modern economy was unsustainable. Natural resources such as fossil fuels were being treated as expendable income when they should be thought of as capital that would one day run out. He also argued that nature's ability to cope with pollution was not unlimited.

Schumacher challenged the idea that growth was good and that bigger was better. Gross national product was not an appropriate measure of human well-being, he maintained. Instead, the aim ought to be to obtain 'the maximum amount of well-being with the minimum amount of consumption'.

Schumacher became a champion of what he called intermediate technology and which later became known as appropriate technology. These ideas were not new. Mahatma Gandhi had promoted small, village-based industries to make local communities self-reliant.

An advisor to the National Coal Board for twenty years, Schumacher went to India to prepare a report for the Indian planning commission in 1963. There he realised that Western economics was the wrong approach to the reduction of poverty in developing countries. It was designed for developed countries and its models had little relevance elsewhere. He quickly discovered that the income of the poor in India could not be raised by following the paths already trodden by Western economies. Building industrial plants in towns and installing the most up-to-date machinery was next to useless because little of the ensuing growth in output would benefit the millions of villages where the deepest poverty was to be found. What was needed was to provide help directly to the villages in the form of training and know-how. The aid-givers, he said, should promote the study and application of simple improvements in the methods of cultivation and related production already in use in the rural areas. By this means, the poverty in each village could be relieved in ways not achievable through a conventional economic approach. There were lessons here for Britain and the other countries that had allowed hubris and mismanagement to reverse many years of progress.

In 1966, Schumacher founded the Intermediate Technology Development Group, which brought together people from all over the world who were trying to improve farming methods. The group set about designing simple methods of improving brickmaking, pottery and other things that were of immediate use. It advocated small working units, communal ownership and regional workplaces employing local labour and resources. Examples of appropriate technology included bike and hand-powered water pumps, the universal nut-sheller, self-contained solar lamps and street lights and passive solar building designs. Since then, even more appropriate technology has developed, helped greatly by information freely available on the internet.

With Britain at its lowest ebb, comparisons were made to the Blitz. But this was different; wholesale death and destruction was absent and people actually began to experience a sense of empowerment as they overcame one hurdle after another. A renewed community spirit was being generated alongside a long-overdue reassessment of life's priorities. For the first time in living memory the phrase 'we're all in it together' not only rang true but meant a great deal to those actively collaborating to overcome difficult problems.

Small is beautiful

With the collapse of sterling, paper money had ceased to be relevant, but basic trade continued by the barter of goods and labour. However, debt had also ceased to be an issue; the systems for collecting money were no more and the slate had mercifully been wiped clean.

People often display enormous resilience in such crises. During the euro crisis in Spain, high unemployment meant that many could not pay their mortgages. The banks foreclosed and evicted them. In 2014 some 3.4m houses were sitting empty, while another half a million had been abandoned part way through construction, products of the pre-crisis building bubble. Waiting lists for subsidised housing became infinitely long and hundreds of thousands of people found themselves homeless. As a result, people broke into repossessed properties, either to live in themselves or pass on to others. It generally cost from €1,000 to €2,000 to 'buy' a repossessed property. Those who could not afford the fee could rent instead for a few euros a month. The deal sometimes even included free electricity, gas and water as Spanish utility workers were not inclined to disconnect those in need. Possession was guaranteed until the bank that had repossessed the house went through the judicial process to obtain an eviction order; a procedure that could take up to two years.

At the same time, many in Greece had abandoned the euro altogether. Older people resorted to bartering, as they had in their youth. This proved cumbersome, so locals set up trading networks, notably in the suburbs of Athens, on the island of Corfu, in the town of Patras and northern Katerini. The biggest was in the cash-strapped city of Volos, 200 miles north of Athens, which had once been a thriving industrial hub with a port whose ferries not only connected the mainland to nearby islands but, before Syria's descent into civil war, had been a trading route between Greece and the Middle East. Once famous for its tobacco, Volos was home to flour mills and cement factories, steel and metal works. But then austerity brought a record unemployment rate of 26%.

To make ends meet, thousands signed up for an informal bartering network using an alternative currency online. Known as the Tem, it was the equivalent of one euro. While the men had their coffeehouses, for women, who were worst affected by unemployment, it became an unofficial support network. Everything from yoga sessions to healthcare, babysitting to computer support were traded in lieu of credits. One advantage of this system was that it avoided the swingeing taxes that had been imposed under the EU bailout plan.

Chapter Four – The Green Shoots of Spring

Once the initial shock of the financial meltdown had passed, people were amazed at how little they actually needed to get by. Food might not have been abundant, but no one was starving. Nothing was being wasted and life had actually become less stressful. Freed from the rat race of the daily commute and pressure at work, morale climbed. Community spirit grew by the day, no one was left out and a functioning society started to emerge from the dystopian world of old.

There had been Utopian experiments at living in cashless societies before. Their ideas and values may have been good, but they often failed due to poor implementation. Ideology could also be a problem as with strong Christian or communist beliefs, there was always a potential for philosophical disputes. They could also be hijacked by a charismatic leader, leading to disaster. Examples have been Jim Jones and the Peoples Temple in Jonestown Guyana or David Koresh and the Branch Davidians at Waco, Texas.

However, when people are thrown together by necessity, they cooperate naturally. During the first days of World War II, almost three million people, largely children, were moved out of the cities in the largest and most concentrated population movement in British history. The children were found billets with families in safe areas that were unlikely to be bombed. British people also helped with money and aid every time there was a disaster. During the 2015 refugee crisis, while governments dithered, people across Europe came forward to help those people fleeing Syria and Eritrea who had washed up on southern shores. Individuals and organisations across the UK offered to house asylum seekers. Under humanitarian agreements, Iceland was only obliged to take fifty asylum seekers a year but in 2015, more than 11,000 families in Iceland offered sanctuary to Syrian refugees. Ordinary people are often more sympathetic to the plight of those in trouble than their self-serving governments.

Britain: Muddling Through

After the collapse, a limited amount of infrastructure was steadily resurrected and, again thanks to the army, fuel was made available for the most pressing requirements. Foreign-owned power stations were commandeered in the national interest. A number of redundant coal-fired power stations had been mothballed, rather than demolished, and were brought back into service. Not with coal as a solid fuel however but as a gas. Underground coal gasification, UCG, had first been mooted in the 1930s and had now been perfected. There were environmental concerns but the overall effect was much less damaging than burning coal above ground. With UCG, coal was partially burned in its underground seams, and combustible gasses – hydrogen and methane – were brought to the surface. This was accomplished without the dirty and dangerous business of sending miners underground to dig it out.

There was thought to be as much as 23trillion tonnes of coal under the northeast coast and the North Sea. This was quickly tapped into for UCG using equipment previously employed to extract oil and gas which, fortunately despite the earlier collapse in prices, was still in place. In addition a number of shale gas wells were drilled onshore. To begin with the gas was used to fire up the old coal plants in addition to the more modern combined cycle gas turbines already in service. In time, the coal plants would be replaced by the newer technology but gas had saved the day. Previously vocal objectors fell silent once they discovered what life was like without heat, light or electricity.

The forces of creative destruction were now in full flow and a new way of life was emerging. Attitudes were changing and minds, institutionalised and subjugated by years of state control, were now exploring new and innovative ways to overcome problems. Only once the entire rotten edifice had actually collapsed did people realise just how much they had lost by allowing a dysfunctional state to dominate their lives. It had been a hard lesson, but at least they now realised that in future they must keep a hand on the levers of power and a much firmer grip on reality.

Lessons from the Past: Scotland and America

A similar situation had pertained in the 1770s, when American colonists grew restive under the corrupt colonialist system. For two centuries, the British had imposed a policy of mercantilism, under which the colonies existed solely for the benefit of the mother country. By various acts of Parliament, the British government sought to regulate the colonies trading directly with other nations to Britain's advantage. This worked well enough when colonial goods were lightly taxed and the colonies lightly governed.

However, that was changed by the French and Indian War (1754–63) that gave Britain possession of Canada, Florida and territory in North America east of the Mississippi, along with St. Vincent, Tobago and Dominica in the Caribbean. But victory had come at a heavy cost and the burden of taxation in England was probably the highest in the country's history. The vast new territory seized from the French had to be defended against various hostile Indian tribes, as well as the Spanish who still controlled land to the south and west. What's more, Parliament had voted to give Massachusetts a generous sum in compensation for its war expenses. The British Parliament therefore thought it reasonable that the American colonies should carry more of the tax burden.

The Americans took a different view. They felt that the new taxes imposed on them – and indeed the whole system of mercantilism – violated their rights as free-born Englishmen. As British subjects, they argued, they were entitled to the same privileges as other Britons. But unlike fellow Britons back home, they were not represented in Parliament and they felt that it was unconstitutional to have taxes imposed on them without their consent. The official British reply was the colonies were 'virtually' represented in Parliament, like most other British subjects. The majority of people in Britain at the time did not actually have the vote but, like the colonists, they were deemed to be represented by those who did.

In 1780 the electorate in England and Wales consisted of just 214,000 people – less than 3% of the total population of approximately eight million. Large industrial centres, such as Leeds, Birmingham and Manchester, were unrepresented. London with a population of 100,000 returned just four MPs, while Cornwall, which was sparsely populated returned forty-four. There were 'pocket boroughs' where a single landlord controlled the voting and 'rotten boroughs' such as Dunwich in Suffolk, which had a population of thirty-two but was still sending two MPs to Westminster as late as 1831.

In Scotland the electorate was even smaller. Before the First Reform Act of 1832, a mere 4,500 men, out of a population of more than 2.6m people, were entitled to vote in parliamentary elections. That was just over 0.17%.

By 1770, there were well over two million people in Britain's American colonies who had no representation at all in Westminster. The colonialists' efforts to assert their rights against a high-handed, dysfunctional and distant British Parliament under the slogan 'no taxation without representation' led to the American Revolution. This was by no means unpopular among the disenfranchised in Britain who made several attempts at armed rebellion that were easily suppressed. One of them, known as Despard's Business, was led by a friend of Admiral Lord Nelson who testified on his behalf at his trial.

During the American War of Independence, the thirteen colonies managed to forge themselves into a new nation. At the First Continental Congress in 1774, the colonies established a representative body. The Second Continental Congress, sitting from 1775, voted unanimously for independence in 1776. Even before the defeat of the British at Yorktown in October 1781, it passed Articles of Confederation, which made the newly reorganised Congress of Confederation a national government.

Once the War of Independence was won, the confederation began to break up as each state asserted its individual rights, albeit with war debts necessitating increased taxes. A convention was called in Philadelphia in May 1787 to decide whether the US should become one united nation or remain a weak federation of autonomous states. The smaller states wanted equal representation in a single chamber, while the bigger states, with their larger populations, favoured proportional representation. The resulting compromise was a bi-cameral legislature with one house – the senate – representing the states equally and a second – the House of Representatives – apportioned by population.

While debates continued, the first draft of a constitution was drawn up. Fearful of the overweening power of the state under the British, it formally divided power between the bi-cameral legislature, the one-man executive – the president – and the judiciary in the form of the Supreme Court. It also gave some guarantees to the individual states.

After compromises were made on all sides, the US Constitution was accepted by unanimous consent of the convention on 17 September 1787 with some delegates, including Benjamin Franklin, disproving of some clauses, but accepting the constitution, 'because I expect no better and because I am not sure that it is not the best'. It was submitted for ratification to the thirteen states on 28 September.

In an effort to persuade New York State to ratify the constitution, a series of eighty-five newspaper articles appeared under the pseudonym '*Publius*' in New York newspapers between 2 October 1787 and 16 August 1788. Most were written by Alexander Hamilton (1755–1804) and James Madison (1751–1836), with a handful contributed by John Jay (1745–1829). They argued that the Articles of Confederation were defective and that the new constitution would mend its weaknesses without threatening the liberties of the people. Later published in book form as *The Federalist*, they address some of the key problems that often bedevil attempts to establish a liberal democratic government in a large and diverse society. These include the nature of representative government, the separation of powers, federalism, pluralism and judicial review. Number 10 discusses the means of preventing factions holding undue sway; number 51 distils the arguments for checks and balances; 70 presents the case for a one-man chief executive; number 78 lays the groundwork for the doctrine of judicial review by federal courts of federal legislation or executive acts.

After the constitution had been ratified by nine states – as required by Article VII – the first elections were held under its provision and the new government took office on 4 March 1789. As ratification in many states was contingent on the passing of a Bill of Rights – based on *Magna Carta* (1215), the English Bill of Rights (1689) and Virginia's Declaration of Rights (1776) – Congress proposed twelve amendments in September 1789. Ten were ratified by the states. These formed the Bill of Rights which was adopted on 15 December 1791. Since then another seventeen amendments have been adopted. This is done under Article V, which says that an amendment can be proposed by two thirds of both houses of Congress, or the legislatures of two thirds of the states. It must then be ratified by three quarters of the states' legislatures or by conventions held in three quarters of them – Congress choosing which method to use. Consequently, the constitution is, to some extent, self-regulating. However, the balance between the rights of the individual states versus the powers of the federal government were still contested and this resulted in a bloody civil war (1861–65).

Despite this, the American colonists did manage to throw off the shackles of a distant and dysfunctional government and, through cooperation, compromise and the exercise of reason, managed to develop a constitution and a system of government that produced one of the most successful nations on Earth. The American experience was to prove invaluable in designing a new 'localised' format for British government which would ultimately avoid splitting the UK into four federal states.

However, the Founding Fathers who formed the 1787 American constitution failed to anticipate the emergence of political tribalism. Rather than the advent of a two party state, they had assumed that politicians would act collegiately for the common good and in the best national interest. It is a moot point that if they had realised that politicians would compete so viciously for power, the constitution would have been drafted in such a manner as to prevent that taking place. Unfortunately, they didn't and the problem of political tribalism was soon to bedevil Britain as well.

Chapter Five – Distant Storm Clouds

Whilst Britain was grappling with its own problems, events were taking a more sinister turn overseas where malevolent forces were at work. Both Russia and China had long connived for the collapse of Western imperialism and plans had been laid. The objective was to broaden their power base and exploit global resources by whatever means possible. To further weaken the West and reduce its ability to intervene, rogue states were used as proxies to destabilise both the Middle and Far East. Israel was attacked by Syria and Palestine using Russian-made rockets and, lacking American support, their situation was dire. Israel had nuclear arms but their use could have produced a cataclysm. South Korea and Japan were targeted by North Korea but neither was able to mount an effective defence due to a massive Chinese military build-up. The UN expressed its condemnation but was powerless to intervene without the armies of America or Europe. Western civilisation was now under attack on both its economic and military fronts and the portents were becoming every bit as ominous as they had been during two world wars.

The Russian Menace

Vladimir Putin showed no sign of relinquishing power. After taking over as acting president of Russia in 1999, then being elected president in 2000 and 2004, he had not been keen to stand down in 2008 when he became ineligible for a third term in office. He endorsed his friend and colleague Dmitry Medvedev in the presidential election. When Medvedev won, he appointed Putin prime minister. After one six-year term – following an amendment to the constitution – Medvedev stepped down in 2012. Putin became president again and gave Medvedev his old job as prime minister back. It was all very cosy. Since then, there had only been token opposition as freedom of the press and public protest was curbed.

It was no secret that Putin was an old-fashioned Soviet hardliner. His parents had survived the siege of Leningrad and he had served as an intelligence officer in the KGB during the Cold War before going into politics. Still a fan of the old Soviet Union, he said he saw nothing wrong with Stalin's treaty with Hitler to carve up Poland and allow the Soviets to swallow up Finland and the Baltic states. He also blamed Britain and France for destroying any chance of an anti-fascist pact, thus allowing the Nazis' rampage through Europe.

On Polish TV, the Russian ambassador blamed Poland for starting World War II by blocking the transit of Soviet troops in the run-up to war – even though Stalin had signed a non-aggression pact with Hitler. The Soviet Union's invasion of eastern Poland, two weeks after the Nazi invasion that had caused Britain and France to declare war on Germany, was not aggression, he said, but a defensive act 'to ensure the safety of the USSR'. It was clear that this was something Russia was prepared to do again, particularly as Putin had rehabilitated the image of Stalin. The political model of the strong authoritarian leader had been restored. Determined to re-establish the Soviet Empire, Putin cancelled elections and was not afraid to call himself 'Диктатор' – Dictator. He sought to bully the former Soviet states, resulting in a war in Chechnya. Putin openly embraced the Orthodox faith as well as inculcating the authority of the Tsar. He was a practised illusionist in addition to a ruthless dictator. There were those who believed his tough exterior hid a pragmatic soul; however most revised their opinion following Aleppo.

Russia's relations with Britain had deteriorated when the UK supported trade sanctions following Putin's annexation of Crimea. Relations came under further strain when former secret agent Alexander Litvinenko died in London after being poisoned with polonium. The UK also gave asylum to Putin's former patron-turned-enemy the oligarch Boris Berezovsky, another of Putin's critics to die in mysterious circumstances. Putin then resumed flights of Russian strategic bombers suspended after the collapse of the Soviet Union. RAF fighters had to intercept these aircraft on a regular basis to defend UK airspace. Meanwhile, his relations with the US also crumbled. Barack Obama cancelled a summit after Putin gave asylum to Edward Snowden, who leaked classified information from the US National Security Agency, before fleeing to Hong Kong.

In 2014, after annexing the Crimea, Putin had also intervened in a Russia-sponsored civil war on the mainland of the Ukraine, seeking to prevent it joining the EU or, more crucially, NATO. With the West in disarray, it was clear that Putin was out to re-establish the old Soviet sphere of influence – and extend it further.

To protect himself from criticism on the web, Putin had a network of pro-government bloggers, while restricting the free use of the internet to others. According to US diplomats, WikiLeaks had revealed that Putin's Russia had become 'a corrupt, autocratic kleptocracy, centred on the leadership of Vladimir Putin, in which officials, oligarchs and organised crime are bound together to create a virtual mafia state'. What's more it launched cyberattacks on Estonia, Lithuania and Finland, while Russian submarines in the Baltic felt free to enter Swedish waters and warn Denmark of the consequences of NATO involvement.

Now that Russia had its forces in Syria, the US and Britain were helpless to prevent the ongoing massacre of innocents in Aleppo. Russia had spent many years and a great deal of money building up the hard left in Britain. Militant unions were funded along with environmental pressure groups and workers' rights lobbyists. Anti-American and anti-Semite groups in particular enjoyed a great deal of support. Russia even operated its own television 'news' channel in Britain, *Russia Today*. Unbelievably *RT* was even allowed to use BBC studios to record programmes and interviews helpful to its cause. A measure of Russia's success is the following extract from the Guardian newspaper. Boris Johnson had urged people to surround the Russian embassy in London in protest at the Russian-backed bombing campaign in Syria which was killing innocent civilians indiscriminately. However, just one protester turned up.

Jonathan Freedland writing in the *Guardian* 14 October 2016:

'Pity the luckless children of Aleppo. If only the bombs raining down on them, killing their parents, maiming their friends, destroying their hospitals – if only those bombs were British or, better still, American.

Then the streets of London would be jammed with protestors demanding an end to their agony. Trafalgar Square would ring loud with speeches from Tariq Ali, Ken Loach and Monsignor Bruce Kent. Whitehall would be a sea of placards, insisting that war crimes were being committed and that these crimes were Not in Our Name. Grosvenor Square would be packed with noisy protestors outside the US embassy, urging that Barack Obama be put on trial in The Hague. The protestors would wear Theresa May masks and paint their hands red. And they would be doing it all because, they'd say they could not bear to see another child killed in Aleppo.

But that is not the good fortune of the luckless children of that benighted city. Their fate is to be terrorised by the wrong kind of bombs, the ones dropped by Bashar al-Assad and Vladimir Putin. As such, they do not qualify for the activist sympathy of the movement that calls itself the "Stop the War Coalition". Indeed, its deputy chair, Chris Nineham, told the BBC's Today programme that his organisation would not be organising or joining any protests outside the Russian embassy because that would merely fuel the "hysteria and the jingoism" currently being whipped up against Moscow. Stop the War would instead, explained Nineham in a moment of refreshing candour, be devoting its energies to its prime goal – "opposing the West".

Despite what Stop the War says, "opposing the West" won't bring any of that horror to an end. For it is Russia that is up to its neck in the blood of Aleppo. It is Russia that joins Assad in the bombing of hospitals. It is Russia which stands accused – and credibly accused –of bombing an aid convoy. It is Russia and its Syrian ally that is fond of the "double-tap" tactic, dropping one bomb and then, after an interval which allows time for paramedics to arrive and start treating the injured, dropping another on the same spot, killing the rescuers.' Freedland went on to add that; '*a spokesman for the Labour leader Jeremy Corbyn expressed his worry that all this focus on Russia "diverts attention" from the atrocities committed by the other outside powers, such as the US – and that it would be just as sensible to protest outside the US embassy as outside Russia's.'*

The 'Stop the War' campaign group repeated claims that many civilian deaths in Syria had been caused by the Americans. Chris Woods of the 'Airwars' monitoring service commented; 'The Russians' death rate probably outpaces the coalition by a ratio of eight to one.' Woods also made the important, but often overlooked, point that while the US and its allies had killed too many civilians – and one was too many – they were at least trying to avoid or limit such casualties. Russia was deliberately targeting civilians and civilian infrastructure.

The Collapse of Global Governance

Syria was yet another example of the Western powers taking and changing sides to suit their own ends or to placate valuable allies. It was a complete mess and one that required a completely fresh approach. However, the human race is at its best under pressure and although nothing seemed to be working many minds were applying themselves to the problems of the Middle East. Israel could no longer count on unswerving support from the USA when President Obama was in office. Its newly re-armed neighbours, long determined to wipe the Jewish state from the Middle East map, knew that they could attack with virtual impunity since, just as in Syria, Israel dare not unleash its nuclear arsenal with Russia backing its aggressors.

The Chinese Menace

China was also bullish. It had new-found client states in Africa. Not only was it flush with a vast surplus of US dollars, it made most of the computing equipment used in the world, making the West vulnerable to cyberattack. It had also cornered the market in rare earth minerals vital for new technologies such as iPhones, wind turbines, electric cars, batteries, robots and precision-guided missiles. There were no substitutes and almost all the world's supply was mined in China.

In an ongoing territorial dispute with Japan, China had built and militarised artificial islands in the South China Sea. Nor had it given up its territorial claims to Taiwan. When North Korea, now armed with nuclear weapons, launched missiles at South Korea and Japan, China made no effort to stop them.

Meanwhile, China and Russia were sharing and cross-referencing intelligence from data hackers in the West. This included commercial intelligence as well as government and military information. The data breach by the Chinese of the US Office of Personnel Management (OPM) affected over twenty million US citizens and included background information for security clearances, detailing people's family ties and contacts, sexuality, debts, affairs, foreign travel, etc. This was a useful database for harassment and blackmail. And, thanks to Edward Snowden, the Russians and Chinese knew everything about the methods employed by the UK and US intelligence service. They not only had a complete picture of what Western intelligence did know, just as importantly, they knew what it didn't know. People's concern about state surveillance quickly evaporated in the face of the genuine security threat posed by the cooperation between Russia and China, and its rogue client state North Korea.

Britain: The Challenge of Reconstruction

But events in far-off countries were now of little interest in Britain as it struggled to get to grips with its own problems. With the threat of outright civil disorder and starvation receding, longer-term arrangements had to be made. Winter would arrive all too soon and heat, power and food would be essential. As much food as possible was stockpiled, fields of low-value biofuel had been ripped up to be replaced with edible crops; even some playing fields and parks did not escape the plough.

During World War II, the 'Dig for Victory' campaign requisitioned waste ground, railway edges, ornamental gardens and lawns, sports fields and golf courses for farming or growing vegetables. Sometimes a sports field was left as it was, but instead of mowing it, the grass was kept down by grazing sheep. Victory gardens were planted in backyards and on the rooftops of apartment buildings. Even Hyde Park had come under the plough. In the twenty-first century, it was possible to go further. Stalks, leaves and other inedible parts of the crops could be fed into anaerobic digesters along with food waste to generate electricity.

The army ensured that there was sufficient fuel for farmers by preventing all non-essential use. Before the crash, Britain had been burning almost 80% of its fuel in commuting, holiday flights and other leisure-based travel. Generally the use of energy in the UK had been coming down, with industrial use naturally showing the biggest decline. Domestic use had shown a slight increase, but by far the biggest growth area had been transport and that was now restricted. With traditional employment in abeyance, few people had the need to commute and holidays were the last thing on their minds.

Currency would be required but what? Sterling now had the status of the mark in the 1930s Weimar Republic and no one would exchange it for goods. The answer was gold; the Bank of England still retained what bullion remained after Gordon Brown's foolish disposal. This, along with rapidly commandeered private holdings, allowed sterling to be re-established on the market, but at only a third of its former value.

Some countries that have problems with their currency use the dollar. But the American economy was also under siege. However, while the UK may not have been blessed with an abundance of gold, it did have great reserves of intellectual talent, particularly in the field of computing, and sterling was soon joined by a new online currency along the lines of Bitcoin. The new electronic currency was called the Turing; the name alone inspired confidence.

As central government was no longer functional, taxes were replaced by local levies to provide essential services. Entire communities prepared for that first winter under their own steam and what had started out as a massive crisis soon became a massive adventure instead.

Lessons from the Past: Revolutionary America

Without central government paying for the armed forces, servicemen found themselves in the same position as American veterans of the Continental Army after the War of Independence. They had been paid in continental currency which had become worthless at the end of the war. On discharge, they had been given certificates for future redemption instead of immediate cash, which hardly helped.

In some states, such as Rhodes Island, the situation was eased by debtors taking over the state legislature and issuing their own paper currency so debt-ridden farmers could pay off their creditors. However, there were court proceedings in Northampton and Springfield in Hampshire County, West Massachusetts, to impound the cattle of farmers who hadn't paid their debts and to seize their land when the grain was ready to harvest.

The veterans organised the farmers into squads and companies to resist this. So the sheriff turned out the militia to defend the court, but most of the militia supported the farmers. They were led by veteran Luke Day, who arrived on the morning of the hearings in Northampton with a fife-and-drum corps after being locked up in a debtors' prison in the heat of the summer.

The courthouses in Worcester and Athol were closed by armed farmers to prevent the courts sitting and taking away their property. In Concord, fifty-two-year-old veteran Job Shattuck, who had fought with the British in the Seven Years' War and against them as a member of the Massachusetts state militia in the American Revolutionary War, occupied the town green with a caravan of carts and wagons and sent a message to the judges saying: 'The voice of the People of this county is such that the court shall not enter this courthouse until such time as the People shall have redress of the grievances they labour under at present.' The county convention then suggested that the judges adjourn, which they did.

At Great Barrington, armed men and boys occupying the town square were confronted with militia numbering a thousand. However, opinion among the men of the militia was split. So the chief justice suggested that those in favour of the court sitting go to the right-hand side of the road, while those against go to the left. Two hundred went to the right; eight hundred to the left.

The crowd then went to the chief justice's home, where he signed a pledge that the court would not sit again until the Massachusetts General Court had sat. After that, the crowd broke into the county jail and freed the debtors. The chief justice, who was also a country doctor, said: 'I have never heard anybody point out a better way to have their grievances redressed than the people have taken.'

The political leaders of Massachusetts, who were largely wealthy merchants in Boston, became alarmed and insisted that the people act within the law – though they themselves had broken the law in opposing the British. But the inhabitants of the town of Greenwich pointed out: 'You in Boston have the money, and we don't. And didn't you act illegally yourselves in the Revolution?'

The rebels began calling themselves 'Regulators' and took a sprig of hemlock as their emblem. The revolt against debt spread to New Hampshire where several hundred men surrounded the legislature in Exeter, asking that their taxes be returned.

The Supreme Judicial Court of Massachusetts met in Worcester and indicted eleven leaders of the revolt for sedition. They planned to meet again in Springfield where they were to be protected by a general with 900 men and a cannon. They were confronted by 700 armed farmers under Daniel Shays, a wounded veteran who had fought at Lexington, Bunker Hill and Saratoga, yet had still found himself in court for debt.

Shays asked the general's permission to parade his men. The general granted it and Shays men marched up and down the square to the accompaniment of fife and drum. Some of the militia joined them while more rebel reinforcements turned up from the countryside. As a result the court was adjourned.

Moves were made to suspend *habeas corpus* and a Riot Act was drawn up. It was read in by the sheriff in Worcester when 160 insurgents appeared at the courthouse. The rebels said they would only disperse if the judges did too. When the sheriff threatened the mob with hanging, someone came up behind him and tucked a sprig of hemlock in his hat. The judges took the hint and left.

As the rebellion spread, Shays marched on Boston with a thousand men, but a blizzard struck and they turned back after one man froze to death. Boston merchants funded an army under General Benjamin Lincoln. There was sporadic fighting, but the rebels were outnumbered. A surprise raid on their camp led to 150 being captured and Shays fled to Vermont.

Hundreds were indicted, but most were pardoned under a general amnesty. Eighteen, including Job Shattuck, were convicted and sentenced to death. Most of the convictions were overturned on appeal, or commuted. Only two hanged. Shattuck and Shays were pardoned by Governor John Hancock, the former American Revolutionist and the first man to sign the Declaration of Independence.

As a result of Shays Rebellion, George Washington came out of retirement and a constitutional convention was called in Philadelphia, which resulted in the formation of a federal government and the writing of a constitution that guaranteed the rights of the separate states – and, later, with the Bill of Rights, the rights of individual citizens.

Britain: Starting from Scratch

Direct action by citizens in America had wrought radical political change and history was about to repeat itself in Britain. Robert Peel, the inventor of modern policing said that British policing was by consent, a theory that would soon be put to the test.

The situation was particularly upsetting for the older generation. The Britain they had grown up in was the undisputed world leader in science, engineering, education and the armed forces; however it had all been thrown away. How on earth had such an accomplished and capable nation allowed this to happen? Historians would one day chart the milestones on its road to decline but a major factor would be its deeply flawed political system that continually and consistently worked against the country's best interests.

The House of Commons was widely referred to as the 'Mother of all Parliaments.' However, it was neither the oldest parliament nor a particularly good example of how a democracy should work. It was specifically designed to promote adversity. It had a rectangular debating chamber, which seated government and opposition MPs directly opposite each other, two sword lengths apart. The theory at the time was that this arrangement would polarise debates, ensuring that governments were held to account. Adversarial debate often produces the best possible outcome and not just in government. It is the basis for making decisions in courts of law, boardrooms and even in family homes. However, when debates become tribal, rather than being based on fact, experience or expert testimony, outcomes are seldom good. Since the professionalism of politics, very little proper debate ever took place and the House of Lords spent most of its time trying to stem ill-conceived, poorly drafted and politically motivated legislation.

Not only did the unremitting need to defeat the other side prevent balanced debate, but MPs were normally told which way to vote before the debate had even taken place. Unsurprisingly this led to increasingly empty chambers; something that became very noticeable when TV cameras first arrived in Parliament. In their defence, it was claimed that MPs were gainfully employed in offices nearby whilst watching the debate on their own screens. Perhaps they were but it didn't alter the fact that important legislation was often formed without being properly debated.

The Palace of Westminster was a historic building but traditions, such as its state opening and Black Rod, gave it an air of authority, stability and gravitas that it no longer merited. Its history had been one of cynical politicking, electoral bribery and wild swings between class-based tribal parties. Over time Conservative and Labour moved closer to the so-called 'centre ground', to maximise their vote. Both parties therefore offered similar manifestos, 'better everything', funded in a manner least likely to upset their own supporters. The charade was becoming increasingly threadbare.

Policymaking was based on chasing votes rather than facts and the results were not difficult to see. Every aspect of our once vibrant country had been compromised by the cynical politicising of the lowest common denominator and electoral bribery. Our economy was heading for a cliff with uncontrollable borrowing and impossible pension commitments, credit card consumerism had replaced manufacturing and many of our services suffered from rank inefficiency and under-capacity. Even worse, lives were now at risk from UK-based terrorists.

Until the Conservative Party sidestepped its own leadership contest in 2016, it had been headed for a similar fate to Labour – being torn apart in a power struggle between the party and its members. However, its reprieve was to be short-lived.

Major reform was going to be needed to bring about government by consensus rather than a never-ending and self-defeating battle with 'the other side'. The problem for political parties was that consensus politics would destroy any justification for tribal politics along with their very existence and these turkeys were not about to vote for Christmas. It would therefore be up to the electorate to take the process now underway to its logical conclusion by collectively and firmly refusing to vote for any candidate standing on a party ticket.

In 2016 there were 650 MPs and all bar one had to stand under a party banner to get elected. Individuals had little chance of competing with hardened professionals, plus a hidden army working behind the scenes. The media, ever mindful not to upset their political patrons, either ignored or ridiculed independent candidates. Parliaments dominated by political tribalism consistently failed to act in Britain's best interests. The case for of overcoming the class warfare that had made the House of Commons into a parody of what a parliament should be was unanswerable. But it would be for the electorate to instigate reform by flooding the chamber with independent MPs.

The UK Parliament was based in the Palace of Westminster, the birthplace of the thirteenth century English Parliament. However, rather than working together for the common good, its MPs were deliberately pitched against one another. This division had traditionally been class based, but now had the added problem of unprecedented borrowing being used to gain electoral advantage. The vast majority of its members had little if any experience of life outside the political bubble. They were also condemned to politically expedient short-term measures by the constant need to campaign for re-election. It would have been difficult to design a more destructive system and the results were nothing short of disastrous.

General elections were marred by electoral bribery, naked populism, doublespeak and political parties offering high-ranking access and peerages for cash. However, the sickness of the system had by now infected the electorate as well. It was plain that many voters were for sale to the highest bidder or susceptible to dog whistle politics. Political parties did not use terms such as 'saving the environment', 'the rich must pay more', 'fairness', or 'the privileged few' without good reason. These phrases were all designed to attract votes from people who had an axe to grind or a perception that others were receiving more favourable treatment than them. The political gravy train also provided a moving feast for the media. Cooperative reporters were fed 'scoops' to give them copy, whereas critical reporters, such as Nick Robinson during the independence referendum in Scotland, were blacklisted, starved of information and even faced calls for their dismissal. Orwell writ large.

Most people soon found that they had no one worthwhile to vote for. All of the political parties had adopted broadly similar platforms, the only difference being the means by which they would raise the cash to pay for their largesse. This meant that few people if any could find a party that reflected more than a few of their views. It was said that politics was a system whereby everyone attempted to live at the expense of everyone else. Never had this been more obvious. However, by cynically bribing people with borrowed money to win elections, politicians had created a country that had become increasingly hostile to living within its means.

It was also instructive to compare voters' knowledge of those who made life-changing decisions on their behalf to their knowledge of those who played games for them. We expended much more time and effort studying the skills and abilities of sportsmen than of politicians. Every newspaper had a sports section based on the minutiae of various games, mainly football, and we were happy for footballers to be paid a great deal more than our MPs. Not only did we tolerate immature behaviour from footballers, we positively encouraged it by supporting a tabloid press that built their empires by reporting the misdeeds and misfortunes of others.

In a society predicated on rights rather than responsibilities, welfare had become a way of life rather than a safety net of last resort. Meantime a bloated public sector effortlessly defeated the best efforts of enterprise to balance the books. The UK was now having to borrow so much money to stay afloat that its citizens had become accessories to the robbery of future generations. Not that this actually registered with very many at the time. Even older people who should have known better were bought off with winter heating allowances, free bus passes, free prescriptions, free TV licences et al. It did not matter if they actually needed these benefits, the grey vote had to be secured and very few of the handouts were refused or returned. Rather than sharing responsibility to make their democracy function as intended, people were now using democracy as a shield to hide behind whilst roundly blaming others for all our misfortunes. Damned if they did and damned if they didn't, the lot of our elected representatives was not a happy one.

By allowing themselves to be taken in by fantasy politics underwritten by unsustainable borrowing, the people had unwittingly put themselves and their children at great risk. They had also undermined the once great society that had united them in common cause and provided moral support. As the state took over more and more of their lives, they had become increasingly disconnected from reality. As a result, people no longer trusted their fellow citizens. Trust had been outlawed and highly-intrusive legislation imposed to guarantee that all possible 'threats' had been minimised. Diversity had become a meaningless soundbite used by government as cover to impose uniformity instead. Philosophers used to refer to 'the tyranny of the majority' when attacking our political system. However, with the arrival of politically correct legislation we soon began to experience the tyranny of the minorities instead. The gay movement often won LGBT groups more rights than heterosexual people. Similarly the highly-organised green movement were successful in having expensive diktats imposed on all, often with little or no scientific evidence to justify them. We had arrived by our own careless hand in the middle of a scene from Animal Farm, demotivated, defenceless and all but de-humanised. Our leading thinkers were silent, unable to map a course back to the real world.

Spurred on by the constant need to get re-elected, political parties had become self-serving fighting machines and the electorate had lost interest. Britain's political system dated from an age when the fastest form of sending information was carrier pigeon. Almost everyone now had internet in their pocket and could be contacted 24/7 yet their representatives only got in touch when an election was due. There were, of course, many 'consultations' especially in Scotland where the SNP played everything from a political angle. However, these were invariably window dressing as the outcomes had been determined in advance. Universal suffrage had become meaningless, reduced to infrequent and one-sided exchanges with professional politicians using misleading gobbledegook. People were now communicating with each other extensively and effectively via social media but still the politicians blocked them out.

Information technology could easily have given the electorate a small part to play in the decision-making process. This would have given people a sense of common purpose and made them more responsive to the needs of others and resistant to the siren call of Scottish separatists and other extremists. The politicians spurned this opportunity, a decision that would cost them dearly. The vast majority of people want little involvement in politics and will tolerate a great deal to get on with their own lives. If the same questions on issues such as education, housing, healthcare and tax, are put to people as far apart as Britain and Australia they elicit similar answers. The needs and aspirations of people around the world are virtually identical and it would have been nonsensical to try and govern different parts of a small island like Britain as separate countries. The rallying cry of Scottish independence seekers was their desire to escape from Westminster's incompetence and hegemony; they were by no means alone in that ambition. Never before had the political establishment been held in such low esteem, and deservedly so. However, this was not just the fault of politicians, the system itself was corrupt. Rather than nationalism, we should have embraced localism and the transfer of more power to communities. Throughout the UK, our town halls stood idle; yet another blunder.

Scottish Problems (2)

It was a combination of factors rather than a single event that kicked off the Scottish devolution process, one of them being Tony Blair. When New Labour swept to power in 1997 it saw Scotland as a potential time bomb. Growing dissatisfaction with the Conservative government in general, and Margaret Thatcher in particular, had given the Scottish National Party a new lease of life. Blair attempted to address the situation by offering the Scots devolution along with their own parliament, originally referred to as an assembly. It was felt that this would shoot the nationalist fox. In true Machiavellian style the Scottish voting system was designed in such a way that an outright majority by any single party was practically impossible. With their dominance in Scotland, Labour considered that they would always be part of the mix in any event, or so the theory ran.

Post 1997, Labour in Scotland failed to mirror its success south of the border. Labour's fiefdoms were moribund and corrupt with many Scots already looking for something better. When Alex Salmond became first minister of the Scottish Assembly in 2007 he renamed the Scottish Executive the Scottish Government and the battle for independence began in earnest. Initially his party concentrated on reversing years of Labour's incompetence, nepotism and neglect to gain the electorate's confidence. Labour was not a hard act to follow and public approval was soon forthcoming. As Labour faltered, Salmond's team grew stronger and many traditional Conservative voters switched to the SNP in the 2011 Scottish election to inflict as much damage as possible on Labour. They certainly did not vote for separation as the question of a referendum was only referred to fleetingly in the small print of the SNP's manifesto. Predictably, the SNP claimed that independence was their entire *raison d'être* and that every vote for them supported for that goal which was manifestly false.

The roots of this problem therefore lay in Westminster rather than Scotland. If the House of Commons had been reformed in accordance with changing times and made more accessible and accountable to the people, then the drive for devolution would probably not have gathered momentum in the first place.

The SNP government published a White Paper in the lead-up to the Scottish referendum titled *Scotland's Future*. It was a superficial blend of highly-debatable assertions and half-truths. A highly politicised document, far removed from a proper White Paper, it was also based on an oil price of $120 per barrel, with projections of it going even higher. If the Scots had voted for independence in September 2014, the plan was for independence to be formally declared eighteen months later in March 2016. Just as with the date for the referendum, this date was selected by the SNP despite Westminster and Whitehall warning that it would be impossible to meet. However having their 'Independence Day' on 24 March 2016 was yet another media-savvy move by the SNP. On the same day in 1603 the Union of the Crowns occurred, when James VI of Scotland also became James I of England and Ireland after the death of his cousin Elizabeth I, while on 24 March 1707 the Acts of Union – which merged the parliaments of Scotland and England – were signed, making one single country, Great Britain. The SNP claimed that the White Paper, at 670 pages and 170,000 words, was the most detailed and comprehensive blueprint for an independent country that has ever been published. At a fundraising event for activists, Scotland's first minister, Alex Salmond, said: 'No nation has ever been better prepared or better researched for independence.' In the event, the Scots wisely voted 'No' and, with the price of oil plummeting to one third of the SNP forecast, narrowly escaped being declared bankrupt on 24 March 2016.

The problem with Scottish MPs voting on English matters was not that the Scots were unintelligent or mightn't have had something constructive to add. An English MP from Cornwall was no more qualified to vote on an issue at Carlisle than a Scottish MP from Dumfries. The issue arose when they were used as pawns by their political masters. Scottish Labour MPs were often used to force through English legislation and the SNP, with fifty-six out of fifty-nine Scottish MPs, was now intent on using Westminster to pursue the break-up of the UK, in open defiance of the 2014 referendum result. SNP MPs not only had to sign an undertaking never to criticise each other in public, they also had to vote as commanded by Nicola Sturgeon who had not even been elected to Westminster. The dangers of combining nationalism with socialism were once again becoming apparent.

As the SNP's focus on independence grew, their proficiency in running Scotland grew less, much less. Not content with packing Scotland's iconic hills with virtually useless wind turbines, manufactured overseas, they lost over £30m backing research into wave power. Even simple things like the need for maintenance escaped them and the Forth road bridge had to be closed to heavy traffic for a number of months due to cutting back on essential repairs. Even worse, when a report suggested that the bridge had a major problem with its cables which would be difficult to fix, the Scottish government quickly decided to build a new bridge alongside it. Labelled the Queensferry Crossing, the new bridge could not handle any more traffic as it was still only dual carriageway.

This is what American comedian Bob Newhart might have made of it if he had quizzed the Scottish government on their latest vanity project.

- *I hear that Scotland is building a new bridge over the Forth. That's an interesting idea, so tell me, how have you guys been getting across until now?*
- *There already is a bridge, ok so why…?*
- *The cables are breaking? Well ok then that could be dangerous.*
- *So how much will a bridge like this cost then?*
- *One thousand six hundred million pounds —that is one heck of an amount surely?*
- *They spent more on the London Olympics, well that must make it stack up I suppose.*
- *Still it does sound like a good way of spending some spare money.*
- *You don't have any money, so how…? Right you're gonna borrow the cash.*
- *A bridge like this is bound to be a good earner right?*
- *No kidding —it's going to be for free!*
- *Still I suppose it will provide masses of local employment?*
- *I see, well the Polish are a fine bunch of people, no doubt about it.*
- *Ok, I am getting it now it's the steel, Scotland is famous for its steel.*
- *All the way from China —you don't say, now that is amazing.*
- *Still you will get a fair bit for the old bridge as scrap I'll bet?*
- *You are keeping it, but I thought? …Oh I see just for buses and wide loads.*
- *Say if you don't mind me asking how did you guys get into this job anyway?*
- *No I can't say that I do understand proportional representation or the single transferable vote system — but they sound like a real hoot.*
- *As a matter of interest what have your bankers said about this idea?*
- *You don't need bankers — so where does the cash come from?*
- *Jeez! Now that is good, you just print it or write IOUs — who dreamt this one up?*
- *You got the idea from the Eurozone? That figures, those guys are wired to the moon.*

- *No, of course I am not anti-Scottish, just expressing an opinion – is that a problem?*
- *And the same to you fella.*

Needless to say, the engineers were able to stabilise the cables on the old bridge and Scotland now had 'a bridge too far'. However, it was just as well Mr Newhart did not turn his attention to the SNP's desire to escape from the clutches of Westminster to submit to the tender mercies of the EU. A bizarre position that many of their own supporters found perplexing, especially after several EU leaders had unequivocally rejected any chance of Scotland being admitted on its own.

Learning to Live within Our Means

So how could we stop political parties bribing voters with their own money and using MPs for their own ends? Any reform would involve giving the electorate more of a say but still allowing MPs to use their better judgment for the common good. Only when we were confident that they were committed to doing just that, could we once again trust and respect them. The internet could help the system to empower those it served instead of exploiting them. Even a small say in certain decisions would transform disillusioned, disconnected and frustrated voters into engaged citizens with a share of the action. One immediate benefit would be the House of Commons becoming a pragmatic debating chamber instead of a Punch and Judy show.

A number of small parties and other organisations, such as the so-called 'Electoral Reform Society', had long been campaigning for proportional representation. However, PR had been trialled extensively in other countries and the results were not good. It simply caused endless back room coalitions with voters having even less of a say. PR did not improve the democratic process, it subverted it. Rearranging the deckchairs on the Titanic would be useless; we would have to go further, much further. The history of the British people had been one of tolerance, responsibility and pragmatism; it would soon be time to find out if they still possessed these qualities.

Strange things were by now happening across the political spectrum but they had a common theme. The old political parties were imploding and, from Brexit to Trump, people were using whatever tools they could find to attack a system that had made them poorer and marginalised them into the bargain. The political elites had become hostages to fortune as years of deceit returned to haunt those who had put their own careers and ideology before the well-being of those they were supposed to serve.

The Labour Party made the fatal mistake of allowing Jeremy Corbyn to stand for leader and his hard-line supporters rapidly made the party unelectable. The moderate wing still had the most MPs and considered forming a new party. However, in the end the rebel MPs fell silent as the enormity of that task struck home. In earlier days they would have resigned to return to their careers and a small handful duly did that. However, few modern MPs had real-world skills to fall back on and they meekly fell in behind their new leader. Labour was finished as a force to be reckoned with for the foreseeable future and had already been wiped out in Scotland.

The Lib–Dems flew too close to the sun and got burned by their coalition with the Tories. There could be no future for them now as a party of protest with only one party to protest about and they lacked the resources to replace Labour as the main party of opposition. They did however propose setting up a new anti-Brexit coalition but leaving the EU was no longer seen as such a major threat and that quickly fizzled out as well.

UKIP won the battle of the referendum but immediately engaged in a bitter leadership contest. Nigel Farage retired and was for a time rumoured to be contemplating the launch of a new party with his main sponsor and friend Arron Banks. Farage was plainly ill at ease with many in his party and went as far as describing UKIP's National Executive Committee as 'amateurs' and 'among the lowest grade of people I have ever met'. However, Nigel Farage was a charismatic anti-establishment figure who would yet play an influential role given his relationship with President Trump.

The Conservative Party held together for a time due to its ruthless capacity for self-preservation. It was helped greatly by Jeremy Corbyn and the collapse of the other parties but had its own problems. The prolonged nature of the Brexit process, with a majority of its MPs for Remain, the strong personalities involved and the unremitting pressure from an ongoing monetary crisis all pointed to extremely difficult times ahead. Although Theresa May tried to follow in the footsteps of Margaret Thatcher, she lacked her certainty of purpose and steely determination

Even the highly-disciplined SNP was by now coming under pressure from its own momentum-style movement, the Radical Independence Campaign. The SNP had gained over 100,000 new, pro-independence members and also moved significantly to the left to sweep up a large body of disaffected Labour supporters. Two groups that soon became extremely difficult to keep onside. The 2015 General Election gave it fifty-six out of fifty-nine Westminster seats but the 2016 Scottish elections saw a drop in support and it lost its overall majority. The splits in the SNP became increasingly fractious including calls for it to ditch the monarchy and form a republic. By 2016, Scotland required cash support of some £300m per week from the Treasury and, even though Brexit had handed it yet another lever to break up the United Kingdom, the future also looked grim for the Scottish Nationalists.

The Dangers of Mob-Rule

The political elite had received an unprecedented mauling but had yet to moderate their condescending behaviour. Professor A.C. Grayling, Master of New College of the Humanities in London, wrote to all 650 MPs urging them not to trigger Article 50 to leave the EU. Professor Grayling justified his call 'made on a personal basis' on the grounds that the electorate had been lied to, the majority was insufficient for a decision of this magnitude and that MPs, the majority who were for Remain, had an overriding duty to act in the national interest. These were valid points and the Brexit campaign probably did exaggerate the benefits of leaving the EU. That said, Remain also exaggerated and was termed 'Project Fear'. Prof Grayling went on to suggest that the EU referendum was a manifestation of 'ochlocracy' or, in simple terms, mob rule. The implication being that Brexit voters were incapable of understanding the issues, a common enough belief in the corridors of power. By this time it had become clear that all the major political parties worked on the assumption that they knew best and the further the public could be kept from the levers of power the better. Thanks to the Lib–Dem-inspired Fixed Term Parliaments Act, the electorate was now only allowed to vote for a change of government once every five years and ignored in the interim.

Credit-fuelled consumerism had changed our economy but it had also degraded our society. Nothing was properly valued anymore and even less got repaired, it got chucked out. Unfortunately this now applied to people as well as hardware.

By 2020 were holding ninety thousand people in overcrowded prisons and, despite the authorities' best efforts, reoffending rates were going through the roof. Those who committed serious crimes had to be imprisoned, to protect the public if nothing else. But when convicts left prison, as thousands did every year, not enough effort was made to settle them back into the community.

We had a reoffending rate of over sixty percent overall and a staggering eighty percent for young offenders. First offending normally resulted from broken homes, peer pressure, poor education and unemployment whereas reoffending was caused by getting out of jail with no home to go to, lost relationships and no prospects of a job. Very few companies would employ an ex-convict but there was one notable exception, Timpson a high street cobbler and locksmith. John Timpson was an enlightened entrepreneur who recognised that making a contribution to society could be financially as well as morally rewarding. *"If we can mend broken objects, shouldn't we at least try to mend some broken people too"* said Timpson, as he began recruiting ex-convicts to work for his company. Timpson had over three thousand employees whom he referred to as 'colleagues.' He also wrote a bestselling book, 'Upside Down Management' extolling the benefits of trusting people and empowering them to run his outlets in their own style.

Within a short space of time some four hundred former prisoners had been taken on, working at cutting keys or mending shoes. Only nine returned to crime. Not only was this an amazing result but these new employees repaid John Timpson's trust many times over with their sheer hard work.

Timpson had proved two things. By successfully employing ex-convicts he demonstrated that people who have strayed are not beyond hope; that they can be just as good and just as useful as other members of society. They may have been damaged and lacking in self-esteem but they were still sentient human beings and not beyond repair. However, the success of Timpson's one thousand plus high street workshops, run on an autonomous basis by their managers, also proved beyond a shadow of a doubt that 'upside down' management was the way forward and devolving power could be a winning formula in the political world as well.

Given that the status quo was falling apart before their eyes, British people appeared to have three options; they could either, (1) give 'intelligent' people more votes than others, first suggested in 1859 by John Stuart Mill in response to Chartists demands for universal voting rights. J.S. Mill however later recanted and said that the *incompetence of the masses* could be overcome if they were given an increased role in the political process, particularly at a local level. A great man and a great pity no one listened to him; (2) they could give up on democracy altogether and elect a president to run the country. They might get lucky and find someone like Lee Kuan Yew who had turned Singapore into a global powerhouse but with the recent upsurge in Corbynism they could just as easily get another Vladimir Putin; or (3) they could learn from John Timpson to give people more of a say and an interest in how their country was run. One thing that had already been a great success, notably in Canada, Australia and Ireland, had been 'peoples' panels.' These were selected at random to make recommendations to Parliament after considering expert evidence and representations from the general public. The sharing of difficult and potentially life-changing decisions made their implementation a great deal more palatable and successful.

One barrier to reform was the perceived length of time that it might take to modernise a centuries-old system where the vested interests still held the levers of power. However, such was the contempt for the *status quo* and the pent-up need for reform that change was now imminent, no matter what. Many had held their noses when voting for Trump but Marine Le Pen would soon follow, the people were on the march. Our leading intellectuals and writers had as yet failed to identify the radical and game-changing measures that would be required. However, necessity is the mother of invention and that 'necessity' was getting closer by the day.

Political parties once had to marshal the opposing forces of labour and privilege but times had changed. Now with less than one per cent of the electorate as members, these relics of the past had lost whatever mandate they once had to control our Parliament. Rather than constantly being used as a means to convey the ideology of whatever political party happened to be in power, parliament would have to become an impartial home for democracy. A permanent institution with rules to ensure effective, responsible and compassionate governance for all and not just the twenty odd percent of those who had picked the winning side. The unrest in Scotland had provided potent evidence of just how unpalatable Westminster had become and not just to the Scots. Unless the British could somehow reform their rotten political system, in addition to economic and societal meltdown, they would also now be faced with the disintegration of the United Kingdom into unsettled factions. The country was at a crossroads. Borrowing was out of control, technology was replacing labour, terrorists were at large and many other challenges lay ahead. However, no government could overcome these challenges on its own. Until the people had become engaged participants rather than critical bystanders, meaningful reform would be all but impossible. Preserving a strong and progressive United Kingdom for future generations now depended on the present generation developing a fit-for-purpose political system to serve its island state. Although the status quo was plainly no longer an option, no one yet knew what would replace it. In the end it was 'learning by doing' that would provide the answer.

Western Foreign Policy: Murder by Remote Control

The Western world claimed to be civilised but the claim did not match the reality. The great civilisations of the past brought benefits to lesser cultures but we routinely tolerated widespread human rights abuse. By failing to help others gain the freedom, dignity and choice that we took for granted, not only had we turned our backs on those less fortunate, but we had jeopardised our own security. Strong measures against the perpetrators of terrorist atrocities were justified but we lacked a game-changing strategy. Rather than continually firefighting, we would have to eliminate the conditions that bred terrorism in the first place. The key would be to agree what human rights were sacrosanct and to defend them across all borders.

We had become skilled at killing people and could even do so whilst seated at a computer thousands of miles distant. However, conventional and primitive means were still being used to massacre innocent civilians by the thousand. So why was it that the powerful armies of the developed world could not simply impose law and order as and when required? Such action was not without precedent and Sierra Leone had been successfully pacified by the British army in 2010. However, mistakes had also been made and we had become risk-averse. Some said that we had no right to interfere in other countries whereas others reminded us that 'the only thing necessary for evil to triumph was for good men to do nothing'.

The Case for Rational Peacekeeping

The biggest obstacle to successful peace-making had been the tension that existed between well-armed countries. Russia was at odds with much of the West, China ruthlessly looked after China, North Korea was a time bomb and nuclear-armed Pakistan corrupt and heavily infiltrated by terrorists. Western democracy was at odds with Eastern potentates, Arab dictators either fought or sponsored Islamic extremists and regime change in Iraq and Libya had provided fertile breeding grounds for murderous fanatics. The willingness of the West to intervene was sapped by failures in Afghanistan, Iraq and Libya, whilst public support for Western foreign policy was undermined by governments kowtowing to brutal regimes elsewhere. A foreign policy based on the politically expedient mantra, 'the enemy of my enemy is my friend' had led us straight into a moral cul-de-sac. It had also sent out mixed messages to both allies and enemies alike. If our military was to be effective, it would have to at least know what it was fighting for.

We were faced with dangerous and escalating situations, some of which had the potential to coalesce into global problems. However, not only were we failing to get a grip on existing conflicts, our grip got slacker by the day. With Western economies on desperately thin ice, defence budgets were constantly under threat and we had grown averse to foreign interventions. We were also becoming increasingly unresponsive to human suffering. Photographs of a drowned three-year-old boy, Alan Kurdi, being carried from a beach in 2015 momentarily pricked consciences and newspaper headlines proclaimed that 'something must be done'. However, little changed and succeeding tragedies had less effect still. Appalling acts of terrorism were now becoming commonplace and had the potential to increase exponentially. We had become guilty of passing responsibility to others. We routinely castigated politicians for failing to act but reserved our most vitriolic opprobrium for when they did but got it wrong. They were damned if they did and damned if they didn't. We used our democracy to sidestep all personal responsibility and the fact that we had elected these people to do our bidding no longer seemed to register.

The war in Syria presented the West with a dilemma. In 2013, the British parliament had decided not to support military action in Syria; or more strictly speaking, it had come up with a non-decision, voting down two separate motions despite a large majority of MPs in favour of action. Shortly thereafter, president Obama quietly shelved plans for military intervention using the face-saving expedient of a Russian plan for removing chemical weapons from Syria. All too soon we were confronted by the harsh reality of what non-intervention meant. Russia used its position to re-establish its hegemony in the Middle East to an extent not seen since the 1970s. President Assad was propped up and the threat to his position removed. The moderates in the Syrian opposition were undermined and the extremists seized the initiative, most notably in the form of ISIS capturing large parts of Syria and Iraq. The modest Western response to ISIS was dwarfed by a large scale Russian intervention which sought to bolster Assad and seemed intent on targeting the Syrian opposition rather than ISIS. Tens of thousands more people died, millions of refugees fled the country and Assad's crude chemical attacks continued. Russia was now in control and took the initiative, resulting in the horrific attacks in Aleppo towards the end of 2016. If intervention had a price, it was clear that non-intervention was not a zero cost option. Following the massacre in Aleppo in December 2016, the National Review said this on military interventions; *"We keep saying "Never again." And then Cambodia happens, and Rwanda happens, and the Balkans happen, and North Korea continues to be a giant maniacal homicidal prison camp. And then the Taliban rises, al-Qaeda rises, and ISIS rises. And then Syria. The world can have messy American military interventions, or the world can have massacres. Those are the options. Pick one."*

President Trump had caused great alarm by making overtures to Vladimir Putin but Trump had made an extremely shrewd choice in General James Mattis as his Defence Secretary. Referred to as 'Mad Dog Mattis' this was a military man par-excellence. Not only did he have a Churchillian grasp of military history, he had the ability to strike fear into his opponents. When the second Trump Putin summit took place in Reykjavik in 2018, the Russian military leaders were presented with a high quality leather-bound diary and a $1,000 bottle of Jefferson's Presidential Select 18 Year Old Kentucky Straight Bourbon Whiskey. However, the generals were less than happy to find that their diaries contained an accurate and comprehensive record of their movements over the past six months. President Putin's movements were also listed in each diary. The threat was unmistakable and its effect was chilling. An affable Mattis also let it be known what his red lines were and the diplomats confirmed that he had President Trump's authority to act autonomously. Putin and his cohorts realised that they had underestimated Trump but they had a problem. Although the Russian military had invested heavily in offensive weaponry, including battlefield nuclear missiles, they had been so sure that the West would never launch a pre-emptive strike that they had neglected to upgrade their anti-missile systems. If Mad Dog Mattis decided to vaporise the Russian high command he would in all likelihood manage to take out the most of them within hours if not minutes. Due to the problems in the UK, General Mattis had also been made acting supreme commander the Royal Navy's nuclear fleet. The skill of RN submariners was legendary and they had outmanoeuvred the Russians on a number of occasions.

A New International Criminal Court

The *status quo* was plainly unsustainable and the longer it continued the more dehumanised, weak and at-risk we became. During the Second World War the Allies had to overcome much tougher enemies. At that time we were up against well-armed nations and gruelling battles were fought by land, sea and air. It was largely a war of machines and if the Nazis had been given more time to develop their rocket programme, who knows what might have happened. This time it was not a war of machines; we were fighting a war of ideologies. Militant Islamists were the biggest threat we faced but they could not be defeated by force alone.

Most people want the same things from life: security, food, a roof over their heads and a future for their children. As Western society developed we achieved more and more for ourselves but elsewhere many were left behind, creating a feedstock for terrorists to exploit. If we could somehow share the freedoms, information, choices and benefits we took for granted with the rest of the world, support for terrorism would wither. Zealots and dictators hold on to power using ignorance and fear. The internet was rapidly overcoming ignorance but we would have to tackle the fear. Not by crusading Christianity but by defending basic human rights.

We claimed to have abolished slavery in the nineteenth century but still countenanced entire nations living under the jackboot. However, the advance of knowledge had raised expectations. We failed to respond to the Arab Spring but change was now upon us whether we wanted it or not. We lacked the moral certitude that we had in 1945, when groups such as ISIL would have been summarily dealt with. However, unless we extended and defended our core values then our 'civilisation' would become meaningless and we would be left with a grim and fear-filled future. For some time now we had taken the easy way out; that option had gone, the enemy was among us and there was work to be done.

However, the sheer horror of Aleppo proved to be a watershed and the West realised that it could no longer stand idly by with impunity. Given the compromised and impotent nature of the UN, a new initiative would be needed. Basic human rights would now have to take priority over sovereignty and religion. Allowing corrupt UN members to veto intervention was no longer an option and the world's liberal democracies would have to unite to get the job done.

The first step was the formation of an International Court of Human Rights, ICHR, based in The Hague. Not only was this a long overdue move, it came as a surprise to many who had assumed that such a court already existed. Although there have been many *declarations* of universal human rights over the centuries, no formal structure had ever been put in place to enforce them. Making core human rights universal would eventually provide the platform required to eliminate global terrorism.

The second sentence of the 1776 American Declaration of Independence reads; *"We hold these truths to be self-evident, that all men are created equal that they are endowed by their Creator with certain unalienable Rights which among these are Life, Liberty and the pursuit of happiness."* The 1778 American Constitution supported that position adding that America should also assist those in need in other countries.

In 1948, the new Human Rights Commission, chaired by Eleanor Roosevelt, the widow of President Franklin D Roosevelt, FDR, drafted the document that became the Universal Declaration of Human Rights. Roosevelt referred to the Declaration as the international Magna Carta for all mankind. It was adopted by the United Nations on December 10, 1948. In its preamble and in Article 1, the Declaration unequivocally proclaims the inherent rights of all human beings: *"Disregard and contempt for human rights have resulted in barbarous acts which have outraged the conscience of mankind, and the advent of a world in which human beings shall enjoy freedom of speech and belief and freedom from fear and want has been proclaimed as the highest aspiration of the common people… All human beings are born free and equal in dignity and rights."* UN members pledged to promote the thirty Articles of human rights that, for the first time in history, had been assembled and codified into a single document.

Although many of these rights have since become law in democratic nations, the UN had singularly failed to enforce them elsewhere. Following the world war against the Nazi-led Axis, countries fighting alongside the Allies were invited to become part of a permanent coalition for peace. When the UN was officially launched in 1945 it therefore contained the seeds of its own failure. Russia and China were accorded permanent member status with the right to veto Security Council resolutions. UN members that do not promote democracy, lest it makes their own citizens less compliant, often veto action against oppressive regimes. With the UN fatally compromised, a fresh start was required. A new organisation referred to as 'Project Peace' was therefore formed but membership was restricted to fully democratic countries. In time most United Nations members signed up to Project Peace with a number remaining members of both organisations until the new organisation settled in.

It was no coincidence that the greatest terrorism emanated from countries with the worst record on human rights. Setting a legally-enforceable minimum standard on human rights for oppressed people was not only our duty it would be the first step to eliminate terrorism. Tyrants and religious fanatics kept their citizens under the jackboot to provide a ready source of cannon fodder. Free people with access to justice and the right of free speech would soon form new priorities, and they would no longer include dying for their oppressors.

Democratic countries required the means to lawfully police errant nations. Sanctions could help but sometimes there was no alternative to boots on the ground. Making core human rights superior to the purported sovereignty of tyrants and religious fanatics was therefore fundamental. To gain the maximum amount of support possible for the ICHR, it restricted itself to assessing just five core human rights as a basis for further action. They were; personal safety, a say in who governed, access to an independent judiciary, a free and independent media and the right to leave. Following a detailed report of human rights abuse from either a democratic government, a human rights organisation or the Red Cross, the ICHR issued proceedings against the errant nation. This gave the country in breach the right to defend itself in court, however given that the complaint was based on human rights that would be regarded as sacrosanct by any rational human being, no country ever took up that option. The court then requested an immediate formal undertaking by the country that it would address these five issues within a twelve month period or face sanctions. If at the end of twelve months sufficient progress had not been made sanctions were imposed and the countdown towards intervention commenced.

The ICHR allowed unsuccessful attempts at firefighting to be replaced with a much more measured and structured approach. Any nation breaching human rights found itself subject to international censure with its position both legally and morally indefensible. By giving detailed rulings, the court helped countries to form a consensus on what types of action were legitimate and thus greatly strengthened the West's cohesiveness. Instead of lurching from one strategy to another, states were now guided by a common set of principles leading to consistent and rational decision-making. All the major religions endorsed the ICHR and it was also supported by the leading relief agencies who had long campaigned for a more structured approach to the world's problem areas.

The ICHR was established with members of the Commonwealth, the EU, the United States and other key allies as founding signatories. A tragedy indeed for millions that it had taken so long. Professional diplomats as well as professional politicians had much to answer for.

If the errant nation failed to respond to sanctions, military intervention was authorised. However, to ensure a successful outcome, much more than just the original five rights was now brought into play. Rather than the UN, the enforcing arm of the ICHR was now Project Peace and it operated under a strict code of practice set out by the Court.

1. The sovereignty of nation states would remain intact unless conflicting groups clearly needed – and sought – political separation or realignment.
2. The religions and customs of other countries would be respected but remain subservient to the original five core human rights.
3. Interventions would be time-limited and subject to a proper process of renewal if this time was exceeded.
4. Interventions would continue until the following criteria were fulfilled;
   a. The rule of law was capable of being maintained by national forces.
   b. The justice system and the media were beyond political control.
   c. Open, free and fair elections were in place to elect governments.
   d. Corruption had been reduced to a tolerable level.
   e. Clean water and sanitation were freely available.
   f. Healthcare was available for those in need.
   g. Education was available to all, irrespective of religion, wealth, ethnicity, gender sexuality, age or ability.

Thankfully the Western world was still capable of forming such a coalition. What remained of its armed forces was well trained, well equipped and highly professional. Its young people were well informed, idealistic and eager to embark on a grand adventure that promised to give their lives greater purpose. What higher ambition could there be than to make a significant and lasting contribution to world peace and prosperity? However, where now for the human race if we had failed to act? Our civilisation had grown weak, introspective and uncertain. We held our leaders in contempt and used our democratic process to shirk personal responsibility. Although our democracy was not perfect, we had to act. A joint effort with our overseas compatriots to deliver peace and prosperity would refresh our society, spark lifelong friendships and provide real and lasting benefit to our economy.

Project Peace's early interventions were areas where organised crime and corruption were the biggest problems rather than deep-rooted religious extremism. Within a few short months, the ICHR had issued warning notices to a number of countries including Somalia, Zimbabwe, Burma, the Congo, Chad and Mozambique. The only option for these countries to avoid enforcement action, which would normally involve economic sanctions followed by military intervention, was for them to agree a timescale to comply in full with the Court's ruling.

Success bred success and, when the far-reaching and significant benefits of the coalition's work began to emerge, more complex and challenging situations came within its reach. It was organisations rather than individuals that were the problem. Once Project Peace had replaced the fear, ignorance and malignancy that sustained these poisonous regimes, with hope, knowledge and an inspirational vision for the future, its work was all but done.

Civilisation: Its Growth, Decline and Rebirth

As history reminds us, civilisations do not stand still, they either flourish or they rot from within. Our civilisation was in steep decline but the majority answered the call as they always do. The UN had become moribund and corrupt and was over time assimilated into Project Peace minus its corrupt member states. Britain had been spending £12bn each year in Foreign Aid. This money had been ring-fenced by the Cameron government, leading to it being shovelled out the door on some extremely dubious projects at the end of every financial year lest it was cut for the following year. Not only was it often spent with little effect or with unintended consequences, much of the funding ended up in the pockets of corrupt dictators or criminals. However, spreading freedom, justice and commerce would provide a dividend far in excess of any cost.

Chapter Six – Creative Destruction on a Global Scale

When new ways of doing things first arrive they can cause upset and alarm until they become the norm. Robots now threatened jobs just as automation once did and even money was changing from something physical to something electronic that you could neither see nor touch.

Despite state interference and incompetence, mankind continued to forge ahead. Uber became successful by figuring out that it was easier to beg forgiveness than to ask permission. It set up shop and then grew its business as fast as possible so that an army of customers would be in place to defend it against the inevitable retaliation by vested interests.

Hillary Clinton had promised to crack down on the gig economy but by the time her words had been uttered she was already too late. With Uber there would be no going back as the ramparts of regulation being used to defend the usual subjects had been breached, giving inspiration to many others. The pace of innovation eventually overtook the growth of government but for a while it was too close to call.

In Britain in the 2020s, the people had come to realise that significant changes could be achieved by direct action at a local level. The scales had fallen from their eyes and no time was to be lost in reforming every sector and system that had been damaged by state meddling and mismanagement. NHS hospitals were handed over to their staff to be run as worker cooperatives. Local subscription provided the initial means with heat and power supplied free of charge. Under the new regime, standards rose and outcomes improved. At the end of the day, matron did not need to return. The staff now had ownership and the staff would protect their patients, their reputations and their livelihood.

Cooperatives had long been regarded as a feature of socialism but all political parties recognised their benefits. Unfortunately, before the crash they had been too busy scoring points off each other to make proper use of them. In areas such as health and social services, where people were motivated by much more than just money, cooperatives were particularly effective as they staff to cope with every eventuality whilst placing humanity ahead of bureaucracy.

This applied in other sectors too. Freed from government interference, education also blossomed. From the first day that pay cheques failed to appear, head teachers had taken control and dedicated teachers, some retired, had volunteered to help out. Here also, standards rose, staff morale soared and autonomous schools settled down to business. They formed linkages with other schools nearby to spread the administrative burden which had been greatly reduced in any event. There was no one now left to send out the endless forms, let alone decipher them, as by now everyone was busy doing something constructive. The way that the teaching profession had been treated by meddling politicians, jobsworths and vested interests was a disgrace. If electricians or plumbers had been dictated to in this manner we would either have been electrocuted or flooded!

Few were left idle in the 'new economy' as there was always a demand for local goods and services as well as helping those in need, the elderly and the infirm. Work was an enabling experience, success intoxicating, and a can-do attitude was now very much in evidence. Freed from mindless bureaucracy, a determination to improve their own circumstances soon translated into direct action. Vacant houses were brought back into service and abandoned factories became centres of enterprise, unburdened by planning control, local authority rates or red tape. Before long, ground was even being taken for new housing as groups came together to share the necessary skills. Local landowners volunteered the ground or it was simply acquired from development companies that had disappeared or gone into liquidation. A highly obstructive and convoluted planning process was replaced by a necessity-based, pragmatic and user-friendly system. In simple terms, if local people decided that they needed to build, alter or do something, it happened. The local economy improved, build quality improved and the few disputes that did arise were settled as quickly and amicably as possible.

One of the greatest American presidents of the twentieth century, Ronald Reagan, once said that the nine most terrifying words in the English language were: 'I'm from the government and I'm here to help.'

However, government meddling and diktat was not just a problem in America. Following World War II, many European governments opted for more state planning, nationalisation and economic control. This era provided the genesis for cyclical recessions and the eventual 2018 meltdown.

In post war Germany, *active and courageous entrepreneurship* 'aktives und wagemutiges Unternehmertum' replaced bureaucratic state planning. Ludwig Erhard, who became

German Minister of Economics, was the father of an economic miracle referred to as 'Wirtschaftswunder'. A staunch believer in economic liberalism, Erhard developed his ideas to rebuild the German economy before the war ended having decided that it would be lost. Erhard viewed the market itself as a social benefit and that the provision of welfare should be kept to the minimum. He was also deeply sceptical of the institutional integration of Europe by the European Coal and Steel Community, an early forerunner to the EU. In 1948, as economic director for the British and American occupation zones, Erhard abolished price controls, despite opposition from the other parties as well as the Allied authorities. Erhard's financial and economic policies soon proved widely popular as the German economy made a miraculous recovery to deliver widespread prosperity in the 1950s. Not only was Germany able to overcome its catastrophic wartime destruction but it was also able to successfully integrate millions of refugees from the Soviet controlled eastern sector.

The quality of German manufactured goods, not least its cars, became the standard by which all others were judged. However, quality was not provided by rules or box-ticking exercises, it came about due to innovation driven by a fiercely competitive marketplace. Germany's progress continued for a considerable period until political do-gooders, extreme environmentalists and a cash-hungry Eurozone eventually pulled it to its knees. Even its world-beating manufacturing industries were crippled or themselves exported by the burgeoning cost of subsidising so called renewable energy systems. In their usual manner, the Germans had put heart and soul into the search for clean energy and named it 'Energiewende' - *energy transition.* However, all the green rhetoric in the world could not compete with low cost shale gas. Although the German government had banned fracking in 2016, it had large deposits which would not to go untapped for very much longer.

Hong Kong, Britain's former island colony off the South China coast was another success story for private enterprise operating within a free market economy. Its success was down to one man, a Scot named Cowperthwaite, 1915-2006. Sir John Cowperthwaite was Hong Kong's Financial Secretary throughout the 1960s and made the colony an international business centre. Rather than a monetarist, he was a classical free-trader in the tradition of Adam Smith, John Stuart Mill and Gladstone. However, he was also a seasoned colonial administrator, noted for his blunt common sense approach. His tactics were simple and he referred to them as 'positive non-intervention.' His achievements in Hong Kong were hailed world-wide as being the strongest possible vindication for a laissez-faire approach. The American commentator PJ O'Rourke called Cowperthwaite "a master of simplicities".

Personal taxes were kept below 15 per cent, government borrowing was not permitted but there were no subsidies or tariffs. Red tape was also reduced to the absolute minimum.

Cowperthwaite believed that government should only intervene to help the most needy and not interfere in business at all. In his very first budget speech he said: *"In the long run, the aggregate of decisions of individual businessmen, exercising individual judgment in a free economy, even if mistaken, is less likely to do harm than the centralised decisions of a government, and certainly the harm is likely to be counteracted faster."*

Another striking example of the ability of a strong leader to transform an economy took place in Singapore. Lee Kuan Yew, 1923-2015, was the outstanding Asian statesman of his time. A formidable political organiser and powerful orator in several languages, Lee became prime minister of Singapore aged 35 in 1959, under the final British governorship. He remained in power for more than thirty years and imposed his austere, incorruptible and often prickly persona on Singapore life. *"I have never been over-concerned or obsessed with opinion polls or popularity polls. I think a leader who is, is a weak leader. If you are concerned with whether your rating will go up or down, then you are not a leader. You are just catching the wind... you will go where the wind is blowing. And that's not what I am in this for."*

For Lee, stability and economic progress far outweighed western notions of freedom. Those who criticised him from abroad often found themselves sued for defamation; those who dared to oppose him domestically were overpowered by every legal means possible. The result was the transformation of Singapore from a mosquito-ridden colonial trading post and military base into a proud and prosperous Asian tiger economy, with the ninth highest per capita income in the world. Although Lee achieved remarkable success by ruling with a rod of iron, this could not solve the problems of a modern world. Not only would people no longer tolerate this amount of top down control but there was now a better option. The journey back to prosperity would begin by giving everyone a say and a share in their own country. Becoming a productive member of a responsible and prosperous civil society would then come naturally from within.

Spanish Troubles

Spain was unable to form a government in October 2015 when neither major party was able to secure a majority of seats in the national legislature. The parties then failed to agree terms to form a coalition so for the first time in its history the country ended up with a do-nothing, caretaker government. While basic government services continued, no new legislation could be proposed, foreign policy was locked and government projects frozen. In contrast to dire predictions of chaos, everything went smoothly and the Spaniards learned a valuable lesson about the resilience of society when left to its own devices.

Felix Pastor, a language teacher, stated: *'No government, no thieves.'*

Mr Pastor went on to say that, *'Without politicians around to inflict more harm, Spain could last without a government until hell freezes over.'*

Ignacio Escolar a website developer agreed:

'A lot of people said we would go to hell if we didn't form a government. But we're still here.'

Ana Cancela, a civil servant, acknowledged the corruption and incompetence endemic to political institutions,

'We already knew that politicians were corrupt, but now we also see that they can't even make politics work.'

Britain Reborn

By now Britain had become the focus of intense media scrutiny. What was taking place was truly remarkable and the outside world wanted to know more. Camera crews combed the country looking for examples of how ordinary people had actually improved their lives following their government's collapse. All round the world, entire nations were glued to their screens watching the drama unfold. What began as simple curiosity soon turned to admiration and then unrest as comparisons were made with the shortcomings of their own governments.

Other countries had long looked to Britain for a political lead. The *Magna Carta* was an influential document worldwide and English Common Law remained the most widespread in the world. Britain was the first European nation to execute a monarch and institute a republic. Norfolk man Tom Paine had influenced the revolutions in America and France. Britain had led the way in the abolition of the slave trade, then slavery itself. Giuseppe Garibaldi and Francisco de Miranda had found refuge in England, as did Karl Marx. He applied for British citizenship but was denied on the grounds that he had not been loyal to the King of Prussia. Lenin later sought refuge in London where he was visited by Stalin in 1905. What happened in Britain was of interest and its twenty-first century revolution soon attracted worldwide media coverage.

What really intrigued observers was the good-natured manner in which these radical changes were now taking place. 'How could there possibly be a revolution without violence and bloodshed?' foreign observers asked. But the British had learned their lesson in the bloody civil war that had resulted in the death of a much higher percentage of the population than even the slaughter of World War I. The result was the replacement of a tyrannical king with a joyless dictator, only to get a king back again in the Restoration.

Though the British cherished freedom, they also valued continuity. Changes had to come slowly, with due deference to what had gone before.

Besides, the British never had much time for dictators. Despite the Great Depression, when much of modern Europe fell to fascist strongmen, the British found the bombast of Oswald Mosley faintly ridiculous. Even in the darkest days of World War II, the British took time out to laugh at Mr Hitler, with *The Great Dictator* becoming Charlie Chaplin's most successful film.

When such huge political changes are made, there is seldom a smooth transition. Normally minorities are blamed – immigrants, Jews or Catholics, as in the Gordon Riots. But this time the British blamed no one but themselves. Those brought up since World War II knew that they had failed to live up to the expectations of the 'Greatest Generation' who had fought it. The British accepted that the national decline since 1945 was their own fault. But that did not mean that they could not still rise to a challenge, possibly even humming *Land of Hope and Glory* to themselves as they did.

Crisis in Korea

While in Britain it was all shoulders to the wheel, in Seoul the government was preparing its surrender to prevent further casualties from rocket attacks from the North. Desperate pleas for assistance had fallen on deaf ears as the few free-world military powers remaining had no appetite for taking on China. South Korea was a small pawn in a big game and had to be regarded as expendable to safeguard their own interests.

The North Korean army of occupation swept South in a long-rehearsed and virtually unopposed manoeuvre. Well-drilled soldiers seized arms and local leaders were quickly identified and rounded up. In an attempt to avoid an international backlash, the troops were under strict orders to avoid the type of extreme brutality they were notorious for. Within twenty-four hours Kim Jong-un was waving to the crowds in Seoul Plaza from the balcony of City Hall. For the first time in sixty years Korea was controlled by a single leader, albeit one who had already become a despot. Kim's first speech in Seoul began in a conciliatory manner. Flanked by his ever-present and watchful generals, he pledged to reunify and strengthen his country promising a bright new future together. However, he then went on to threaten all-out war against *'an evil America and its running dog allies.'*

North Korean troops quickly discovered that they had conquered a country whose people were wealthy beyond belief. Not only did they all have motor cars, most families had two or three of them. They also found that they were physically smaller than their former countrymen. Years of malnutrition with every available penny being spent on the military had taken their toll. They shared a common language and a common history with the south but, more significantly, they often shared family names and ancestors. Fear and hostility were soon replaced by curiosity and relationships began to be formed. A small gift of food to a patrolling soldier, a furtive conversation or a shared photograph and the tension began to ease. This did not go unnoticed by the generals who decided that this rapprochement had to be stopped before it got out of hand. They were also concerned about the amount of information that their troops were picking up. South Korea had world-class information technology and everyone had internet access. Web access was now being blocked but that did not erase knowledge or material already downloaded and the troops were daily becoming more aware that they had lived their entire lives in a poverty-stricken and oppressed vacuum. However, the ruthless generals soon figured out how to re-impose their authority.

A popular and well-known South Korean figure was seized from the street, accused of being an American agent and plotting against the 'liberators'. His home was raided and weapons and explosives, which had been planted earlier, were put on display for the media. Also on display was 'evidence' of a North Korean soldier supplying information on troop movements and army installations. In fact, the soldier's only crime had been to voice concern about some of the more extreme violence that had been inflicted on his countrymen. But that was enough to single him out and another arrest was made.

The show trial was a foregone conclusion as was the death sentence handed down on both men. Suddenly, the tension was back with both sides about to be given a brutal reminder of the power held over them. The execution would be by machine gun in the Plaza with Kim Jong-un in attendance. The entire population of Seoul between the ages of twelve and seventy was ordered to attend and, with few daring to stay at home, a huge crowd began to gather at first light. The people were afraid but they were also resentful. Their restlessness soon became apparent and the troops grew nervous. North Korean martial music was being played through the public address system but, as the time approached, this was matched by another type of music. Activists had set up a small transmitter nearby and the haunting melody of the Korean national anthem Aegukga began to swell from hundreds of handheld devices throughout the Plaza.

Suddenly all eyes were upon the balcony where Kim Jong-un had appeared flanked by his grim-faced generals. At precisely ten o'clock the two doomed men were led out in manacles, blindfolded and placed with their backs against City Hall. An execution detail of four special force troops marched smartly in and took up position facing their two targets. Kim began to speak but no one was listening. A murmur of dissent quickly swelled to a roar of protest and the crowd surged forward to engulf the firing squad and form a protective shield around the two terrified men; the generals had waited too long.

The scene was now set for a massacre and all eyes again turned to the balcony, anticipating the inevitable order to fire, but it was deserted. Something, the earlier fates of Ceausescu and Gaddafi perhaps, had panicked the dictator and the sound of a helicopter grew louder. However, it was by now too late as his own men had turned on him and Kim Jong-un was never seen again. The episode ended with troops and spectators hugging and cheering madly. The war was over and victory was clear but this time it was the invaders that had been liberated.

The Death of Dictatorship

If events in Britain, now being copied throughout Europe and America, were inspirational, what had just happened in South Korea was incendiary. The implications were not lost on other repressive regimes or those they controlled. After centuries of bloody conflict and oppression, the world was at long last gathering itself to move in a new direction.

Christians had not triumphed over Muslims, democrats over dictators, left over right nor secularists over theists. At the end of the day, it was the sheer volume of information getting spread by the unprecedented force of the internet that had released ordinary human beings from the shackles of ignorance and fear. Common humanity, crossing all borders and encompassing all races was in the ascendance. It had taken centuries and there had been many bloody setbacks along the way but it was about to become a unifying and unstoppable force for good.

Groups such as Daniel Barenboim's West–Eastern Divan Orchestra with musicians from countries in the Middle East, of Egyptian, Iranian, Israeli, Jordanian, Lebanese, Palestinian, Syrian and Spanish background had paved the way. The speed and ease of the internet, formerly used as powerful channel for terrorist propaganda, was found to be even more powerful when used as a power for good. Vast empires carved out by the likes of Facebook and Twitter, though banal in content, brought people together. They allowed people to express themselves promptly and to a wide audience. Personal disputes and ideological battles were now being resolved in a pragmatic and sometimes even cathartic manner. Once the poisonous effects of political tribalism began to diminish, sworn enemies became close friends and people began to regard their fellow man in a much more positive manner.

Chapter Seven – A Brave New World, At Last

By the 2020s the world had already undergone great change but was still evolving. Just as neighbour had rediscovered neighbour, countries and continents were now rediscovering each other and rejoicing both in the diversity and the commonality they were identifying. Different races, creeds and religions were finding out more and more about each other by sharing knowledge, doing business or just simply making friends. Foreign holidays were no longer based in tourist enclaves, as getting to know the local people and their customs was far more rewarding.

Within living memory, only the wealthy, emigrants and those posted to far-flung quarter of the empire travelled. Holidays, such as they were, were taken at the seaside. Then in the 1960s came package holidays. Initially, these offered cheap flights and accommodation in the Mediterranean. As time went on, destinations became more exotic and the whole world fell within reach.

The internet then arrived and supercharged the entire process. The days of having to sign up for a pre-packaged holiday from a tour operator were over. You could now go online and tailor a holiday to suit every aspect you wished with almost all destinations and facilities already having been thoroughly reviewed by those who had gone before. Accommodation provided by companies such as Airbnb meant that holidaymakers did not find themselves stuck in a hotel with other travellers; they could now live with the locals instead.

This quickly became a two-way process and countless friendships, bonds and long-term relationships were forged. As well as socially, the world was now racing ahead in breaking down scientific, engineering and technical barriers as well. Cutting-edge technology was no longer the exclusive preserve of giant corporations or the military.

Urban centres across the globe introduced citywide free Wi-Fi allowing people to travel more and work wherever they found themselves. Budget airlines thrived and young people, often after being enthused by a gap year, adopted a nomadic lifestyle. In the absence of terrorism and security checks, travel became so easy and carefree that it soon broke down all remaining barriers between races, countries and religions. In time even passports were abandoned. We were all One World citizens now.

The internet was developed during the Cold War so that, if one pathway between computer systems was broken, another would be found. The worldwide web was then created to distribute the enormous volume of data that was coming from the CERN European nuclear research laboratory to universities and research institutes around the world. As the Large Hadron Collider increased in power, it generated so much data that a new superweb had to be developed. As a result, the Open Source Movement flourished. With the whole world swathed in the web, it was no longer possible for large corporations to enforce copyright. So on the internet at least, there was a level playing field.

Now that the need for commercial secrecy and military supremacy had been virtually eliminated, the best minds were applying themselves to mankind's greatest needs. The forces driving innovation were no longer cash or waging wars; they were improving living conditions, helping the young, healing the sick and forging local, national and international relationships. However, the most powerful innovation of all was internet access now being provided free of charge on a global basis. Thousands of new satellites, relay stations and transmitters now beamed high-speed broadband into the remotest areas and many millions of receiving devices had also been handed out.

The spread of mobile communication made life more difficult for any would-be dictator. Stalin was terrified of the telephone, realising that if people could have covert conversations it undermined his power. Throughout the communist era in East Europe the ownership of photocopiers was restricted. Consequently, writers distributed their pamphlets and novels by having them retyped by trusted friends. Mikhail Bulgakov's novel *The Master and Margarita,* and the essay *The Power of the Powerless* by dramatist and dissident Václav Havel were circulated that way. Dissident copyists had to use carbon paper to produce more than one copy at a time. However, after the fall of the Berlin Wall, Havel became president of Czechoslovakia.

Fax machines also became a useful tool in the hands of those who opposed dictatorial governments. When pro-democracy students occupied Tiananmen Square in Beijing in 1989, the fax was a vital means of communication with the outside world. The Arab Spring, the Orange Revolution in the Ukraine and the Rose Revolution in Georgia all took off because of mobile phones and the social media. Unfortunately, the social media also helped coordinate the riots in England in 2011 with MI5 noting that terrorist plots that once took months or even years to plan could now be organised via the internet in a matter of weeks.

Overall the impact of the new technology was positive and power was decentralised. An outsider, such as Barack Obama got himself elected, not by putting himself in the pockets of wealthy paymasters and corporate sponsors, but by crowd sourcing. Some governments did fight against the web to retain control over their citizens and blocked access to a number of websites. Internet users' traffic was also monitored. Bloggers were hired to pump out propaganda and opposition parties or groups were hacked. However, they were in a losing race with a population that was quickly finding ever more sophisticated ways to mine the mother lode of information that the internet offered.

A New Mainstream Media

These events transformed mainstream media as well. Where once economic trauma, terrorism, despotic dictators, corrupt politicians and scandalous celebrities had dominated the headlines, positive news was now the order of the day. People no longer accepted what a sensationalised media told them and, robbed of revenue, many of the tabloids went out of business. Following the press-hacking scandal which saw one editor jailed, a public inquiry was held by Lord Levenson. However, his eventual report, suggesting stricter controls on the press was only welcomed by those few that had been hacked in the first place. Most people wanted the press to be able to search out corruption by any reasonable means and most major scandals were in fact uncovered by investigative journalists. These ranged from MP expenses, bribery of FIFA officials and Russia covering up its Olympic drug abuse. The eventual solution was simple. Just as every other service was now rated by websites such as TripAdvisor and Gocompare, all newspapers were also now rated and had to publish their scores on the front page. National newspapers were judged by a specially selected panel on veracity, relevance, impartiality and public interest. The top three newspapers were given an annual award. Not only did the new competition drive up standards but it had a massive effect on sales as well. Few people wanted to be seen reading or even buying a newspaper that was rated little better than a comic so not only were people better informed, sales returned to a level not seen for many years. Just as book sales had quickly recovered once people tired of electronic reading, newspaper sales recovered once people realised that they could once again trust the printed word.

However, for the rapid dissemination of information and news, the internet now had no equal. When a massive earthquake devastated Haiti on 13 January 2010, the news circulated on the net at lightning speed, eliciting an instant response. Social media had raised $8m by the end of the first week and ReliefWeb provided an online portal for those trying to help. The website Digiphile used search technology to relay posts on Twitter feeds, coming from a fifty miles radius of the earthquake, to direct rescue teams. The disaster unfolding in Haiti no longer seemed so distant.

Meanwhile the propaganda pumped out by the state-owned media of North Korea and other dictatorships had been replaced by real reports and, given recent events, it was all positive. There were no restrictions now on the worldwide web and it was the perfect tool to help mankind knit together as a cohesive body. A collective mind-set was developing and its driving force was the desire to reach out and cooperate with others. The old order had at long last yielded, making way for the new and it was unlike anything so far experienced. Even countries which had avoided the worst problems were all too aware of the oppression and traumas suffered by others and quickly signed up to the new order.

In the UK, the political landscape was transformed and the old tribalism had gone. General elections were also a thing of the past and MPs were elected, recalled or retired on an individual basis by popular demand expressed via online polls.

Before, lightweight MPs had struggled to manage events, sometimes with disastrous if not lethal results; the national debt was rising by almost £3bn every week and opposition parties were in total disarray. The 2016 Cameron-led EU negotiations were both shallow and exclusive with no real opportunity for the electorate to express any opinion other than 'Yes' or 'No'. This, despite the long-awaited referendum being possibly the most important political decision they would ever have the opportunity to make.

Lifting the Curse of Party Government

The common factor in all of the above, and much more besides, was the party system. Political parties were a construct of factional and widely divided sectors of society seeking to influence events for their own interests rather than the common good. Even after the ancient divisions in society had all but disappeared, politicians continued to cynically use class warfare as a weapon. As a result, the system was hardwired to work against Britain's best interests, to exclude the best people and to incur levels of debt that could never be repaid without massive currency devaluation.

In the lead up to the 2018 crash, our leading philosophers, political analysts and commentators were ominously silent about the future, albeit they had plenty to say about the past. In 2016 Hillary Clinton was destined to become the first female president of the

USA, the EU referendum would be in favour of Remain and the main UK party of the 20th Century was on course to continue its dominance well into the 21st. By early 2017 the only survivor was the Tory party but not for much longer. Given that the biggest single party now in the UK was 'none of the above,' our political system was doomed.

Political parties sowed dissent as their very existence depended on them splitting the electorate into competing camps. The only way to end to this ruinous process would be to get rid of them altogether, we had tested tribal politics to destruction. What we now needed was a system whereby our representatives sought consensus rather than conflict. A revolution was sweeping through the Western hemisphere as electorates rejected the parties that had failed them. What followed would need to be success-orientated, inclusive and robust.

Political parties and movements promoted conflicting ideologies. They ranged from centre ground mainstream parties, adjusting their policies to maximise their votes, to more extreme movements such as Trotskyists and neo-Fascists. So far the centre had prevailed but only by managing decline at the expense of future generations.

Faced with worsening personal circumstances and turned off by constant mud-slinging, voters had become alienated. Many did not vote or voted for what they regarded as the least bad option. As a result, the Conservative Party was in power with the support of just 24% of the electorate, the Scottish National Party with 26%. Three quarters of the people had not voted for the government of the day and the writing was on the wall.

Most people were perfectly capable of getting on with their lives without engaging in constant disputes with their neighbours. Political tribalism had only endured thus far because the electorate had lacked a viable, non-tribal option to vote for. The grip of the parties, aided by a compliant and news-hungry media was too well-established. What the people actually wanted was an effective, consensus-led administration, rather than a never-ending power struggle between warring factions.

So what was so different about our needs and aspirations that we required different political parties to represent us in any event? Most people looked for security, a roof over their heads, a proper education for their children, access to healthcare, employment and perhaps even the opportunity to better themselves. In other words, precisely what was supposedly on offer from *all* the major parties. It took a child to point out that the king had no clothes and any child could have told us that, heads or tails, we were going to lose whichever side we picked in this futile battle.

The establishment fought the challenge to its stranglehold and the media, dependent on never-ending political intrigue for copy, defended it. But the ramparts had been breached with Donald Trump changing the game out of all recognition. Trump may have been anathema to many but he was no extremist. However, many of those now appearing from both ends of the political spectrum were far from innocent. We had a clear choice: we could either reform our political system so that it became fit for purpose, or we could stay with the status quo and give the extremists an open goal.

Some spoke about forming a new political party. A party that would listen to its voters, use the internet to involve its supporters, be more responsible with our money and promote localism. However, unless we were prepared to accept a single party totalitarian state, that wouldn't have worked either. Just as people adapt to changing circumstances, so did politicians. After this 'good party' had enjoyed a brief honeymoon, realpolitik would reassert itself, the electorate would be again be offered bribes and the vicious circle would return with a vengeance.

The only chance the electorate had was to refuse to vote for party candidates altogether and flood parliament with independent MPs instead. If the House of Commons could be freed from the machinations of political parties, it would function properly and work for us rather than against us. That said, independent candidates could not compete against large professional organisations that sold political access to fund their campaigns. A £6 million fund had therefore been provided by a group of philanthropists to successfully overcome this problem during the 2020 general election. This stimulated an equal amount of crowdfunding and given the anti-establishment mood, a majority of independent MPs were duly elected. This sent out a strong signal and many of the MPs that had been elected under a party ticket resigned the whip to join them. The tyranny of political parties was thus brought to an end. This however left the long-standing problem of how future political campaigns could be funded so that poorer people and minority groups did not get excluded. The answer was for local people to pick their own candidates and have their campaigns funded by the public purse. To maintain healthy competition, a local selection panel, themselves appointed by ballot, picked the best three candidates in each constituency, with the incumbent MP being allowed to stand as well. All candidates then received equal campaign funding which they were not allowed to top up and the winner was elected by the single transferable vote system. State funding therefore ensured that even those of limited means were able to stand and local selection panels were responsible for ensuring that all candidates were selected on merit alone. To ensure that MPs did not form cabals to overcome fair debate, simple anti-trust rules were also enacted. As for the ideologues; they were left to fight it out amongst themselves in smoke-filled backrooms, the rest of us had lives to lead.

America: Government by Faction

Political tribalism, was long ago recognised as a potential source of trouble. When the US Constitution was ratified and the First Congress convened in March 1789, there were no political parties. The first president, George Washington, had no political allegiance. However, Congress soon split between federalists under Alexander Hamilton, who favoured a strong united central government, close ties to Britain, a centralised banking system, and close links between the government and men of wealth, and anti-federalists, who became known as Democrat–Republicans, under Thomas Jefferson and James Madison. This was a matter of regret to Jefferson who wrote in 1798: '*Two political sects have arisen within the US; the one believing that the executive is the branch of our government which the most needs support; the other that, like the analogous branch in the English Government, is already too strong for the republican parts of the constitution; and therefore in equivocal cases they incline to the legislative powers: the former of these are called federalists, sometimes aristocrats, and sometimes Tories, after the corresponding sect in the English Government of exactly the same definition: the latter are styled republicans, Whigs, Jacobins, anarchists, disorganizers, etc. these terms are in familiar use with most persons.*'

Initially, the vice-president was the runner-up in the presidential contest, so President John Adams, a federalist, had Thomas Jefferson, a Democrat–Republican, as his vice-president. Jefferson was also the presiding officer of the senate, giving him the tie-breaking vote in case of a deadlock. Republican Abraham Lincoln's vice-president in his second term was Democrat Andrew Johnson, who succeeded after his assassination, until he lost the next election to Republican Ulysses S. Grant.

Britain: Whigs and Tories

In the UK, the party division initially came about because of the Exclusion Bill of 1679. This sought to exclude the Duke of York from the succession because he was a Catholic. In the seventeenth century to British Protestants, 'Popery' was synonymous with arbitrary power wielded by an autocratic monarch, enforced by a standing army – as in France and Spain. These things were anathema to free-born Englishmen, particularly those who had fought against, defeated and executed the despotic Charles I, who had married a Catholic and was thought to harbour Catholic sympathies. Those who opposed the bill were called Tories; those who supported it were Whigs.

The bill passed the Commons, but was rejected by the Lords. Charles II then dissolved

Parliament and reorganised it so that his supporters, the Tories, held powers. The Duke of York succeeded as James II, but was deposed in the Glorious Revolution of 1688. Although the Tories and the Whigs cooperated in the removal of James, the split between the parties continued with the Tories favouring the Anglican Church and the monarchy, while the Whigs supported the supremacy of Parliament and Nonconformism. Although the parties were rejigged a little over the next three centuries, that essential split continued into the early years of the twenty-first century.

Britain had been a two-party state since political parties first appeared. Until the 1850s politics in the United Kingdom was dominated by the Whigs and the Tories. These were not political parties in the modern sense but loose alliances of individual interests. The Whigs included many of the leading aristocratic dynasties committed to Protestant succession and later drew support from the new industrialists and wealthy merchants. The Tories were associated with the landed gentry, the Church of England and the Church of Scotland. The Tories evolved into the Conservative Party, and the Whigs into the Liberal Party. In the late nineteenth century the Liberal Party began to pursue more left-wing policies causing many traditional Whigs to move to the Conservatives. The Liberal and Conservative parties dominated the political scene until the 1920s, when the Liberal Party declined in popularity. It was replaced as the main party of opposition by the newly formed Labour Party which represented an alliance of workers, trade unions and socialist societies.

The campaign for all to have a vote finally succeeded in 1918 when the Representation of the People Act gave the vote to all men over twenty-one and to all women over the age of thirty. In 1928 women were also given the vote at twenty-one. The Chartists fought and died for this right but in the end their triumph became a Pyrrhic victory. Rather than using their newfound power to seek out the best people to represent them, the fledgling electorate were persuaded to vote for parties instead. By derogating their power to parties the electorate inadvertently put their trust in organisations that would seldom act in their best interests. However, the people now had someone to blame if anything went wrong. Since then, a great deal had indeed gone wrong but this flawed arrangement had proved so debilitating and addictive that it had become set in stone. It may have seemed a good idea at the time, but the abrogation of responsibility along with power would return to haunt us.

In their constant quest for power, political parties broke every rule in the book. They abused the rights of their staff, operated cartels, bribed and routinely misinformed the electorate, and they incurred levels of debt that could never be repaid without massively devaluing sterling. However, their success in setting one half of the electorate against the other eventually proved to be their undoing. Labour focus groups when presented with a range of Conservative policies, without being told their origin, often praised them but would reject them if informed beforehand of their provenance. The same applied to Conservative focus groups with Labour policies. The politicians were caught in a swamp of their own making.

An MP's lot was not a happy one. Imagine the scenario; a nationwide company is interviewing an executive for a highly responsible and demanding job.

Interviewer: *'The salary is not all that good but you will have an expense account. However, be careful as the rules on expenses are complex and a dodgy claim can get you into really hot water. You will be subject to intense scrutiny at all times, even on holiday, and your friends may be offered bribes by the media to spill the beans on you. We will need full disclosure on every source of income you have and this will be published on the internet for all to see. You must also keep a record of everyone you meet, especially those who wish to discuss company business. Unless you are invited to sit at the top table, which is highly unlikely, your opinion will not be taken into account but you must always support the company line when required. Oh, and I almost forgot, you will need to reapply for your job every five years, possibly sooner.'*

Candidate: *'Goodbye.'* It goes without saying that any commercial enterprise run on these lines would quickly go bust, and deservedly so. Yet this is precisely how the UK attempted to run its government. Because of a few bad eggs, all MPs were treated with such contempt that the skilled people the country so badly needed would not come forward. As a result, the only people entering politics in recent times had been those with no real-world experience. We had driven away the very people that we really needed and this became an ever bigger problem as the crisis deepened.

Ending the National Health Service

Evidence of state-run cartels was provided by the NHS, i.e. the 'Nationalised' Health Service, closely followed by state education. All political parties paid homage to the NHS by guaranteeing its funding and forswearing privatisation. Scandal after scandal rocked it to its foundations but still successive governments failed to grasp the nettle. One of the worst took place in Mid-Staffordshire in 2008 when a much higher than normal mortality rate in patients admitted as emergencies rang alarm bells. When the NHS Foundation Trust responsible for running the hospital, failed to provide an adequate explanation, a full-scale investigation was carried out. Released in March 2009, the report severely criticised management and detailed appalling conditions and inadequacies at the hospital. Press reports suggested that, because of the substandard care, between 400 and 1,200 more patients died between 2005 and 2008 than would be expected for the type of hospital. This figure was hotly disputed by NHS officials. It was also estimated that upwards of 5,000 unnecessary deaths were occurring every year due to hospital acquired infections caught in NHS wards. Despite its failings, the NHS had skilled defenders who mobilised rapidly whenever a perceived threat appeared. Its most entrenched supporters were opposition parties who did not need to fund it and a multitude of vested interests. It had 1.7m UK employees, 1.3m in England alone and provided a dripping roast for a wide range of supply companies. However, by far the biggest stakeholders in the NHS were the sixty-plus million people who depended on it, often in life-or-death situations. Yet their needs were brushed aside by those who would defend it right reason or none. If patients had actually been the prime consideration in dealing with the NHS, then the ballot box would have forced reform many years before it eventually took place.

As well as being politically sacrosanct, the NHS also commanded a great deal of mystique. Many people seemed to believe that it did something unique that could not be bettered. However, the NHS did not create the health service, it merely nationalised it in 1948 and the first NHS hospital did not appear until 1964. Its hospitals, equipment and medicines were all provided by the private sector. The private sector also practised in all its specialities and shared many of its consultants. The only real difference, apart from accident and emergency, was that the private sector was properly managed and readily available. It was also a great deal more cost effective. In 2016 the annual cost of the NHS was around £1,780 per capita and full-blown private medical insurance would actually have cost less. The answer would therefore be to utilise private sector acumen whilst still providing essential healthcare free at the point of need.

Getting a Real NHS

Aside from wealthy individuals paying their own way, private healthcare was normally accessed via medical insurance. A number of enlightened employers provided this facility as an incentive to their staff. Many trade union leaders, public sector employees and politicians also resorted to private healthcare whilst hypocritically denying it to others. Rather than the state trying to run the health service itself, the logical solution was to provide means-tested private medical insurance to all who could not afford it themselves. Existing NHS hospitals continued to provide services on demand, being paid for services delivered rather than by block grant. A major advantage of blanket healthcare being underwritten by third parties was the freedom from political interference this gave frontline providers. It also transferred responsibility from politicians by making service providers properly responsible instead. Yet another highly successful measure, prevented from being implemented years previously by political point scoring.

Curbing the Lawyers

One of the problems that had brought the NHS to its knees was the huge number of claims made against it. The barrier to launching legal action was low and law firms took on cases on a 'no win no fee' basis but grabbed the lion's share of any subsequent pay out. Compulsory mediation provided the solution and had long been mooted for the NHS. However, this had been constantly stymied by gravy train lawyers misusing human rights legislation.

Farewell to Red Tape

Another serious problem had been the imposition of the EU-inspired Working Time Directive on NHS staff from 1 August 2009. This caused a wide range of problems. Patients suffered from a lack of continuity as shifts changed, and senior clinicians complained bitterly about the lack of time-related experience being acquired by their juniors. On-call doctors had their duty time recorded even when they were fast asleep. Once again legislation introduced to improve matters had backfired and coroners had even mentioned the lethal effects of this legislation in their reports. However, the Working Time Directive was no more and the wards returned to normal.

Democratic Education

State education was also in trouble, especially in Scotland, and displayed all the classic symptoms of a failed nationalisation. However, it also remained locked into a destructive time capsule by those using it to further their own careers and political ideology. Despite the usual weasel words, political parties had always put their own interests ahead of those of pupils and patients. Members of the government did however use private hospitals and sent their children to fee-paying schools. As state schools got worse, more parents had scrimped and saved to send their children to private schools. These schools had long been the preserve of the upper classes and this embedded class division. Due to connections made in these schools and the quality of the education provided, their pupils went on to dominate law courts, large companies, Parliament and even sport, art and the stage. The class barriers had been gradually breaking down but were now returning and the supreme irony was that this was being caused by the very system that was supposed to give everyone equal opportunities: state-funded education. So desperate did the politicians become to achieve this goal, they even demanded that universities accept less qualified students from poorer backgrounds to artificially skew the figures in their favour.

Given the sheer volume of bureaucracy and the cast of thousands weighing down the state sector, it soon became apparent that it would be a relatively simple matter to provide better quality education at a lower cost. Following years of studying and starting low-cost private schools in Third World countries, Professor James Tooley opened one in Durham. Professor Tooley's no frills school offered 'a traditional education focusing on an academically demanding curriculum, hard work and good behaviour.' The fee was just £2,700 per annum and the school was soon fully subscribed. This concept also helped to address the well-documented problem of parents failing to take an active interest in their children's education and classroom misbehaviour. Although state education collapsed not long after Professor Tooley opened for business, his school provided a first class example for others to follow.

When the shackles of the state were removed, it was easier for pupils to become more engaged with their own schooling. They found they could help teachers decide on what subjects they were taught and how. Headmasters were free to introduce new disciplines and innovation rapidly replaced mindless bureaucracy. They lost no time either in dealing with substandard teachers who were either retrained or let go. Taking a lead from fee-paying schools, some pupils asked for the reintroduction of classics. Others sought inspiration in the arts, where Britain was already an acknowledged world leader. Children were also keen to emulate the great Britons of the past and eagerly embraced the rigours of science, technology, engineering and mathematics. Looking outwards to the world, there was a renewed interest in learning languages – particularly Mandarin, Cantonese, Urdu, Hindi and Arabic.

Parents who had been sending their children to fee-paying schools were delighted to return them to the state sector once standards had recovered. The left had long aspired to close down private schools altogether, accusing them of embedding social division and giving unfair advantage to those who could afford to pay. Wealthy parents were also aware of the problems caused by social division but their main priority was for their children to have a good education. There had been no private schools in Germany as the state sector was so good. Parents who used fee-paying schools, however, were not just paying once, they were in effect having to pay twice as school fees were non tax-deductible. However, rather than the state funding the schools directly, parents were given school vouchers instead. To be completely fair, these were means-tested so that the wealthiest parents were still paying but now they were only paying once and their children had a much more rewarding time at school as well. To get results, fee-paying schools had worked their pupils very hard and the pressure had at times simply been too much, robbing many youngsters of a proper childhood.

A Classless Society

Despite the best efforts of certain political dinosaurs, the old class divisions had faded helped by modernisers under Tony Blair. The moderate, Blairite, faction continued to control the Labour Party until the sudden election of Jeremy Corbyn as leader. Although he was popular among party activists and many new members had signed up to support his candidacy, he was not popular with other members of the Parliamentary Labour Party. These were people who realised full well that the electorate would no longer support hard-line socialism although many Labour MPs privately shared his views. Corbyn only passed the threshold of thirty-five nominations from other Labour MPs because twelve members who supported other candidates lent him their vote to widen the debate. They were aghast when he succeeded in being elected leader. The Labour Party whip became an anachronism as its MPs followed Corbyn's own example of defying it at will. A number of Labour MPs resigned including Tristram Hunt, himself a onetime leadership contender. A large number of rebellious Tory Eurosceptics soon began to follow Labour's example as the Brexit negotiations progressed. As party discipline broke down, MPs from other parties began to follow their conscience and a worn out and discredited system began to creak in earnest.

Whilst Jeremy Corbyn could only count on the support of a handful of left-wing diehards, he still had an important constitutional role to play. As a privy councillor, he had stepped into the shoes of Tony Benn. A rank anti-monarchist, Benn had worked out a legal way to rid Britain of the monarchy. In the unlikely event of a bill abolishing the monarchy being passed in Parliament, it would not receive the royal assent. However, Benn pointed out that the heir to the throne did not automatically inherit the crown. Since the Glorious Revolution, the new monarch had to be invited to take the crown by a unanimous vote of the Privy Council. As a privy councillor Benn said that, if he outlived Queen Elizabeth, he would vote against Prince Charles – or whoever else was put forward – ascending to the throne. Benn did not outlive the Queen but, as Leader of HM Opposition, Corbyn became a member of the Privy Council and, except in exceptional circumstances, membership was for life. As Benn's vicar on earth, Corbyn intended to vote against the succession, preventing any new monarch taking office. This would have been yet another politically fatal manoeuvre for Corbyn but by this time no one was counting. In his own way, Jeremy Corbyn did much that helped bring about the end of a thoroughly worthless political system. That may not have been his intention but we should be grateful in any event.

It was the power of patronage that had allowed political parties to control their MPs with a rod of iron. The leader of the political party that won the general election became the prime minister. They then selected their favoured MPs from within the ranks of their own party to act as Ministers and form a government. Patronage provided the base for political power but strangled democracy and initiative as dissenting MPs were denied promotion and never made it into the cabinet. However, as the political revolution gained momentum, spurred on by an impatient electorate who had by now scented blood, this changed. There was no way that they were going to tolerate 'their' MPs being ordered about by others. At the same time, following the Jeremy Corbyn debacle, it was clear that MPs were best placed to choose who became a minister and even who became prime minister. In June 2010 an important change was made to the procedure for appointing select committees. All appointments had until then been made by parties with the winning party controlling most of the committees. From 2010 however these committees were appointed on a cross-party basis from the floor of the House. The quality of the work performed by the committees was greatly improved and this model was duly used with remarkable success for all ministerial appointments.

Following boundary changes, the House of Commons could now choose from 600 MPs to form a government but they were henceforth going to be chosen for their ability rather than their subservience to any political party. Cabinet responsibility was still in evidence but exercised in a manner to deliver the best possible outcome for the country as a whole rather than political point scoring.

Towards True Democracy

Another glaring democratic deficit had been the inability of constituents to deselect or recall their MP if they had misbehaved or went against their wishes. Once again this had been something that had been talked about for many years but nothing was ever done. In 2014, to honour part of the 2010 coalition agreement, the government tabled a Recall Bill but it did not give the power of recall directly to an MP's constituents. Instead, an MP would only face a by-election if 10% of constituents signed a petition, *after* the MP had been found guilty of 'serious wrongdoing' by the Parliament's standards committee. Only if the MP had been sentenced to more than twelve months in jail was the matter placed directly into constituency hands. They would also be given the option of calling a by-election if their MP had been banned from the Commons for more than twenty-one days. However, with the standards committee composed entirely of MPs, twenty-one-day bans were unlikely ever to be handed down.

In October 2014 Conservative MP Zac Goldsmith tabled an amendment to the Bill which would have excluded the Parliamentary Standards Committee from any role in determining whether errant MPs should face re-election. However, in the time-honoured spirit of self-preservation, MPs rejected the idea by 340 votes to 166 following a free vote in the Commons.

Speaking during the four-hour debate, Mr Goldsmith urged MPs to put aside concerns about the technicalities and cost of recall elections and focus on the principles instead:

'What is at stake now is a matter of principle – do we trust our voters to hold us to account or not?

'The public today is better informed, better educated, less deferential than at any time in our history. Recall is not radical – it is a mere nod towards those changes.'

MPs from all sides used weasel words to praise the bill but voted down the Goldsmith amendment which would actually have made it meaningful. For example the Constitution Minister Sam Gyimah pledged instead to look at a new Lib–Dem proposal to create an additional 'trigger' process outside of Parliament but alongside the internal process. More meaningless flannel to keep the public happy but, as with the Chartists, reform could only be delayed not stopped altogether.

When recall was finally introduced it followed the Canadian model by opening an annual window in each constituency for a vote of confidence. If more than 10% of constituents sought recall, a by-election was held with the sitting MP allowed to stand if they felt they had been unfairly treated. In return, MPs were given ten-year terms before having to stand for re-election, attractive salaries and a commercially proven and private system of expenses. This linked MPs firmly to their constituents but gave them a much more rewarding and stable workplace in return. It also restored a modicum of privacy and dignity, the lack of which had been a solid barrier to excellence. In addition it solved the old problem of the majority of voters not getting the government they had voted for. Henceforth MPs were directly answerable to their constituents and there was a collegiate government chosen on merit alone.

No More General Elections!

In an even more radical move, general elections were scrapped altogether. The purpose of general elections was to hold governments to account by changing parties but they had degenerated into 'bribe fests' to get votes. General elections were also hugely time-wasting and disruptive. Preparations for them did not begin a few weeks before they took place, they began immediately after the previous election had been won. Five years of campaigning with politically motivated, short-term decision-making and the parties constantly jockeying for position via their chums in the media. Then as the election proper drew near, all work stopped and Parliament became even emptier than usual as its members took to the streets to shake hands and kiss babies. Post-election, not only did the entire government, including its prime minister, have to change places overnight, but the relationship between ministers and their department was also severed. This regular bloodletting subverted democracy by giving an entrenched civil service the upper hand against a procession of unseasoned ministers. Once political parties had disappeared, it made a great deal more sense to have a permanent parliament with its component parts being held accountable instead. The parliamentary term became a settled and productive continuum marked only by the constant check and refreshment of its members. The House of Commons moved from political chicanery, short-term fixes and mediocrity to become an institution all could be proud off. The views, needs and aspirations of ordinary people were now woven into the fabric of Parliament rather than being cynically exploited for votes. MPs were once more held in high regard and accomplished and talented people again aspired to enter the political arena. The knocka-bout and aggressive style of politics was replaced by a productive chamber which spent the greater part of its time stripping out the superfluous legislation that had accumulated over the years. The electorate played a major role in getting rid of bad legislation by way of a new, Wiki-style, website called *Unintended Consequences*. Anyone who had been at the receiving end of poor quality legislation, producing negative rather than positive outcomes, could now put its problems online for all to see.

These turned out to be the most radical, democratic and positive changes since the signing of *Magna Carta* in 1215. However, they had been achieved by ordinary people making a collective decision to drive out the old ways. Needless to say, if left to their own devices, politicians, aided by the enormous media and public relations gravy train that they supported, would have done and said anything to hang on to power.

Government by National Consensus

Once political parties no longer existed, the House of Commons operated by consensus. Politicians still argued their case with passion but the mindless insults had given way to informed and inspired debate that many now tuned in to watch; changed days indeed.

As the long overdue reforms began to take effect in the House of Commons, concerns were expressed about the possibility of independent MPs forming groups, or cabals, to have a particular policy adopted or another prevented from becoming law. Given the positive mood now infusing the House, not to mention the constant presence of TV cameras, this was not considered to be a major threat. However, it did make sense to future-proof reform by requiring all MPs to sign up to code of practice with penalties for non-compliance. The following protocols were therefore enacted.

1. All policy making shall be carried out in plain sight, either by debate in the Chamber or in open discussion in Committee, having due regard for issues of a confidential or sensitive nature.

2. No MP shall accept a commission, paid or otherwise, from a third party to influence the opinion or behaviour of fellow MPs unless any such commission is recorded in the procedural register.

3. Any MP found to be in breach of these rules by the Standards Committee shall be subject to sanctions including an unlimited monetary penalty, expulsion from the House or have a by-election ordered in their constituency.

These measures would guarantee the future of good governance. Parliamentary Privilege was designed to prevent MPs being hindered or unduly influenced from outside parliament however most of the interference came from within.

In this way continuity prevailed, the will of the people was honoured and minorities respected. The old-fashioned bidding war of electoral bribery was replaced by a much more pragmatic and performance-driven system. Confrontation faded into the background as politicians stopped stirring up class warfare to concentrate on making essential services as user friendly, efficient and cost effective as possible. Vast amounts of mindless legislation had also been scrapped as people were no longer prepared to be treated as potential criminals or fools.

Taxes were simple, regulations light and public sector spending only accounted for twenty percent of the budget now that all the state monoliths had either been mutualised or closed down. The day of the professional politician was gone and our government had at last become a government of the people, for the people by people of proven ability. The 'Mother of all Parliaments' had cured its sickness and once again gave a clear lead to the rest of the world. Where Great Britain had failed to impose democracy by force, it now succeeded by example as other countries rushed to copy its reforms. The abolition of political parties in the UK was soon copied by other European countries. America also followed suit having grown weary of year-long hugely negative election campaigns funded by billionaires. However, the federal system was retained as it was well-suited to combining the freedom of localism with the ability to pool essential resources.

Chapter Eight – Glorious Summer

As the British now had time to appreciate the finer things in life, the arts flourished. History once again became important in an effort to understand and learn from our downward spiral and mistakes made. The bible also gained new followers among those committed to lead more inclusive and meaningful lives. Organised religions had all too often adapted the scriptures to suit their own purpose and congregations had dwindled. However, Christian and Islamic writings still had much to offer a modern world. A few fundamentalists continued to preach intolerance, but their audience soon drifted away to more enlightened messengers.

Although the British people had long considered themselves to be a spiritual race, church attendance had slumped as materialism flourished. While most people believed that there was something deep and mysterious behind the universe, there was less support for a lord set above us whose language and imagery borrowed directly from feudalism. Even many otherwise-committed Christians, while finding their inspiration directly from the Bible, refused to be bound by the hard-and-fast dogma of the established religions.

An Islamic Reformation

The move towards Islamic fundamentalism was reversed as a new generation of Muslims grew up. Just as the deracinated sons of West Indian immigrants sought identity with Rastafarianism, the second generation found it easier to fit with the conventional British way of life. So second-generation Muslims flourished in mainstream life. This movement – as with the offspring of West Indians – was led by the young women. Muslim girls seized the opportunity to enjoy the clothes, the make-up and the freedoms of their white sisters. And where the girls went, the boys were sure to follow. However, one development was especially helpful – a new version of the Koran was produced by enlightened Arabic scholars. This greatly ameliorated the language of the Quran in much the same way that the New Testament had softened the fundamentalism and intolerance of the Old Testament.

The production of a new version of the Koran was given a long overdue kick start in 2016 when a Pakistani born British Muslim, Paigham Mustafa, published a book which gave others the courage to put their head above the parapet. *The Quran: God's Message to Mankind* set out to challenge the perception that Islam condoned violence against non-Muslims, domestic violence and polygamy. The book also questioned the interpretations that required women to cover their faces and that honour killings could be justified. Mustafa claimed that that the original Koran had adopted a much more pragmatic and civilised position on these issues.

The publisher and businessman was forced to seek police protection in 2001 after a fatwa was issued by 15 imams accusing him of spreading "sedition" and "satanic thoughts" in the magazines that he produced for the Muslim community.

He then spent more than a decade researching the earliest known texts of the Koran and exposing wilful misrepresentations. Mustafa showed that the peaceful and inclusive message of the original text had been hijacked over the centuries by errant religious leaders for their own ends. In his book, Mustafa posed the powerful question: *"If Islam is true, why then are Muslims in such a despicable state? Muslim countries are some of the least developed, the poorest, the most corrupt and the most tyrannised in the world."*

He called on *"Muslims, intellectuals and all people who want a better world to critically analyse and evaluate the whole of the 'Islamic' tradition, not only from the past 200 years, but even the millennia before that. And in this evaluation there must be no place for sentiments and prejudice."*

In 2001, a written fatwa was circulated in thousands of leaflets among Muslims in Mustafa's home city of Glasgow comparing him to Salman Rushdie, himself the subject of a fatwa by the Iranian government in response to his book The Satanic Verses.

Mustafa was ostracised by family and friends and forced to withdraw from public life to such an extent that he even had to miss his father's funeral due to threatened violence.

The father of three, who was raised a Sunni, knew only too well that by publishing his book, he was putting his life at risk. Earlier that year Asad Shah, a Glasgow shopkeeper, had been stabbed to death by a fellow Muslim who accused him of "disrespecting" Islam. An imam from Rochdale was also battered to death by an Isis-supporting Muslim who accused him of practising a form of healing he deemed blasphemous.

Mustapha claimed that he was both a believer in the Koran and a humanitarian but the holy writings had been distorted to enforce views detrimental to society. *"I'm doing this because I believe in the word of the Koran and it troubles me that it's being used falsely to justify, not only terrorism and violence, but a whole range of practices that are harmful and unnecessary and that are destroying people's lives on a daily basis.*

"Strictures regarding how women should dress and behave, the demonising of homosexuality, widespread practice of polygamy, the ritual of slaughtering animals for food and a ban on alcohol consumption are not justified according to the strict word of the Koran.

"Governments in the UK and other western countries are seeking to engage with so-called 'moderate' Muslim leaders to tackle extremism but, in many cases, they are part of the problem. These leaders shake hands with politicians while, behind their backs, they are committed to doctrines of hate."

Although he was the only person living under a fatwa in a western country at that time, Mustapha's courage bore fruit and the scholars duly rose to the challenge.

Some who rejected empty secularism found comfort in Sikhism, which combined the teachings of Islam and Hinduism and offered a positive and inclusive identity for those who saw their roots in the subcontinent. The Baha'i faith also flourished because it sought to embrace other all other faiths, rather than seeking the ascent of one over another.

A (Better) New World Order

The old world orders of communism, socialism and capitalism had been and gone, all failing in their own way; communism and its little brother socialism by failing to trust or empower the people, and capitalism by allowing the division between rich and poor to grow too great.

Communism had effectively met its end with the fall of the Berlin Wall although its death was protracted and painful. Many of the former Soviet satellites had become members of the European Union and NATO. Although Vladimir Putin had clamped down on some of the worst aspects of the free-for-all capitalism that followed, his new authoritarian and crooked government made no attempt at redistributing wealth or power in the interests of the people. Ever the diplomat, even at 92, Henry Kissinger made the following observation on president Putin; *"We are worried that his objective is to destabilise the West. He is worried that our objective is to undermine him."* Putin however suffered a mortal blow when the CIA posted a full inventory of his cash, looted treasures and secret properties on the internet. The Communist Party still nominally ran China along Marxist principles, but the system was essentially state-sponsored capitalism. But then, Karl Marx himself said that he was not a Marxist.

The Communist Party still ruled Cuba but this was changing. Since the collapse of the Soviet Union, they had been cut off from Russian sponsorship and the Cuban government had to open the island to tourism to get cash. Following the Obama rapprochement and the death of Fidel Castro, American tourists poured in. For years, Cubans had sought to escape poverty and repression on makeshift rafts and small boats, attempting to cross the Straits of Florida to the land of plenty they had seen on MTV. Now they had dollars in their hands without risking their lives.

The Democratic People's Republic of Korea had ceased to exist and Korea was once again united. The Koreans of the north had endured an even harsher time than Eastern Germany under the communists. However, having discovered that they had not actually been living in a 'socialist paradise while the rest of the world lived in the squalor of poverty and oppression', they were now eagerly looking towards a completely different and bright future.

Capitalism was also changing. It had not destroyed itself as Marx had predicted. He thought that as factories got progressively more efficient, fewer people would be needed to own and run them, forcing more of the bourgeoisie into the working class and thereby making revolution inevitable. Capitalists, such as Henry Ford, realised however that it was in their interests that their workers were paid well. That way, they had money to buy his products. Bill Gates and Steve Jobs followed suit. However, there was a yet another change in the digital age. Many of the products in the marketplace were actually computer programs and other forms of digital information that could be reproduced easily and cheaply. This meant that the price mechanism which had formerly kept a balance between the scarcity of a product and the amount you could charge for it no longer applied.

The great corporations found that they had to retain the goodwill of the public by acting in a socially responsible manner. They could not withstand a sustained onslaught in social media if they were not seen to be playing the game and paying their taxes. Leading entrepreneurs followed the example of Rockefeller, Getty, Guggenheim, Peabody and J.P. Morgan, who had spent their vast wealth in philanthropy and endowing public institutions. This set the stage for Bill Gates and Warren Buffett, who pledged to give away 99% of his fortune, primarily via the Gates Foundation. Wealth was now flowing freely from the rich to the poor without the coercion of punitive taxation and consumer goods were priced as low as possible.

The new world order was instinctive, strong and inclusive, a combination of the Enlightenment and the Renaissance. The spread of knowledge and social media had allowed mans' instinctive humanity and goodwill to overcome the dark forces which had flourished in our midst. Mutual respect, forgiveness and understanding were now intuitive and international. The new order might not have been Utopia but it was probably as close to that fabled citadel as the human psyche would ever permit.

Legalising Drugs

Now that the majority had at last accepted responsibility for their own destiny, a vast, complex and self-defeating collection of petty laws had been cast aside. The market in recreational drugs plummeted as ambition returned and real-life experience overtook mind-altering drugs. Society was no longer dysfunctional, props were not needed and people 'got high' on their own achievements. This had a welcome knock-on effect in countries such as Afghanistan and Mexico. The farmers still grew their poppies but the heroin now had a legitimate analgesic market and the drug barons had melted into obscurity.

Many countries followed the example of Portugal which had relaxed its drug laws without widespread problems. At last, the world began to learn the lesson of prohibition, where banning alcohol had simply put its supply in the hands of the criminals.

Ironically, the United States was the hardest to persuade to follow this path. They had begun the banning of drugs with the Shanghai convention in 1909 in an effort to dent the British Empire which was profiting from selling opium in China. After the hiatus of World War I, other drugs – such as cocaine and marijuana – were banned under international treaty. However, the position of the Federal Government was undermined in the early twenty-first century when other states followed the example of Colorado and began decriminalising the possession of marijuana. After all, it was not nearly as dangerous or addictive as the new synthetic drugs such as MDMA or crystal meth.

Mexican drug barons had originally dealt heroin after the growing of opium in Sinaloa Province had been encouraged by the US during World War II. Having had its supplies cut off when Japan invaded China and Burma, the US military needed morphine for its wounded soldiers. The Mexican drug cartels took over the trade in cocaine and marijuana after the American Drug Enforcement Administration had cut off the supply routes across the Caribbean, giving the Mexican crime lords a monopoly on transhipment. But with decriminalisation in the US and other parts of the world, the price of formerly illegal drugs collapsed. This meant that – rather than risk having their crops destroyed by the DEA – the growers in Latin America, Afghanistan and elsewhere got a better price selling their produce for legitimate medical use, rather than to criminals who took most of the profit.

People were now much happier as they reaped the benefits from being part of an active society that valued their input. Everyone was now a great deal better off as well. Firstly they were more affluent as the state soaked up less cash. To sustain an enormously bloated public bureaucracy, taxation had become extensive, complex and ruinous. However, the taxation system was now so fair and simple that adequate funds were ingathered without protest or avoidance. The principal levy was a flat tax with no banding to discourage hard work.

The Reform of Taxation

In 1974, at a meeting with Dick Cheney and Donald Rumsfeld, the economist Arthur Laffer sketched a graph on a napkin to demonstrate the effect that the rate of tax had on revenue. Laffer demonstrated that at either end of the possible tax band no revenue was generated. At zero per cent tax, no revenue but at 100% also no revenue as no one would bother working. Laffer reckoned the most effective tax rate was around one third, 33%. At this rate, people would not only be encouraged to work hard, being able to keep the lion's share, but no one would waste time trying to avoid paying tax. Also present at this meeting was the associate editor of the *Wall Street Journal* Jude Wanniski who coined the term 'Laffer Curve'. President Reagan immediately saw the force of this argument and famously increased revenue by cutting taxes. His example was successfully followed by Margaret Thatcher and then President Trump who wisely combined it with stripping out a great deal of over-regulation in the financial sector.

Wealthy people were normally skilled at manipulating the tax system, or could afford clever accountants to do it for them. It made sense to pay an accountant well, if they were going to save ten, twenty, a hundred times the amount in tax. However, as well as cutting tax rates, tax law was greatly simplified as well. Entire volumes of small print drafted to close thousands of loopholes were replaced by one law, the Rule of Primary Purpose. In any dispute with the tax authorities, consideration was given to specific measures adopted by taxpayers. If it was found that a company or individual had adopted a specific course of action with the sole or primary intention of evading tax, then the benefit was disallowed. There was of course the right to appeal but such was the opprobrium now reserved for those trying to avoid paying their fair share that few appeals were ever made.

The super-rich had always used complex methods of protecting their wealth but most no longer bothered, they were after all human beings. Not all were driven by making money in any event, although few liked to see it wasted. Wealthy people were also excited by the new world order, especially for the sake of their children. Children of wealthy parents can all too easily be unbalanced by seeing money splashed around and become spendthrift if given too much spending power before maturing. The new order had opened up societies around the globe and money was no longer the key to accessing life's best experiences.

Even ordinary people who would go to great lengths to cheat the taxman, if they thought they were being treated unfairly, would pay up if they thought taxation was reasonable. When income tax was introduced, some argued that it was unethical. People should not be taxed on what they earned for their hard work, but rather on what they spent. The revenue from a sales tax was self-regulating. If the tax is increased, the price of the goods rises, so sales will fall. But then, an individual could decide whether to buy some, and pay tax, or go without and avoid the tax. However, this was itself unfair as it meant poor people paying the same level of tax as wealthy people on essential goods. This was recognised when Value Added Tax was first introduced by exempting essentials such as food, clothing and shoes. However, as incompetent governments became increasingly short of funds, very few exemptions survived. The Labour Party swept to power in 1997 on the back of a promise not to increase income tax or corporation tax. They did keep this promise but increased every other tax instead, including VAT. New Labour also introduced a bewildering array of new 'stealth' taxes. Legitimate environmental concerns in particular were cynically exploited to raise more revenue. Labour's Gordon Brown and Ed Balls were skilled at introducing levies under the pretence that they would benefit the environment rather that the Exchequer. Naturally the opposite happened. The Climate Change Levy was quickly followed by such gems as the Aggregates Levy, Carbon Levy and Air Passenger Duty. To begin with these levies were offset by reductions in the rate of National Insurance Contributions, to make them 'revenue neutral'. However, immediately it was judged safe to do so, the higher rate of NIC was restored with a bit extra for good luck. Value Added Tax had been a major tool for every Chancellor since it was introduced as a result of EU harmonisation in 1973. It started life at 10%, dropped to 8% under Denis Healey who also increased it to 12.5% on 'luxury goods' including petrol. By 2016 it was at 20% and much of this was levied on items that had to be bought from income that had already been taxed. Chancellors used to announce percentage increases in VAT in terms that were less than honest. An increase from 15% to 20% was presented as a 5% increase when in fact it was actually a full one third increase, 33%. Double and even treble taxation was rife. This became so bad that if a working man bought a gallon of fuel for his car for £6 the Treasury actually pocketed £8.70 in revenue. The worker had to earn £8.50 and pay

£2.50 in income tax and PAYE to have the £6 to start with. There was £2.63 duty and £1 vat on every gallon, oil companies paid a 50% higher rate of corporation tax. When you considered the tax paid by oil workers, tanker drivers and forecourt staff it all added up to an awful lot more than most people realised. It was said that the main difference between the Mafia and the Treasury was that the Mafia actually understood the Laffer Curve. Once taxes were simplified and lowered, additional revenue also arrived from the demise of the black economy. Not only were traders keen to become legitimate but their customers also now insisted on paying them by traceable means rather than cash.

It was well known that both David Cameron and George Osborne were keen students of Tony Blair whom they referred to as 'The Master.' However, less well known was just how many of the former Labour leaders' methods they routinely used. Perhaps the sneakiest of all was a process Blair referred to as 'triangulation' whereby you make a great show of supporting one course of action in public whilst doing something completely different behind the scenes.

As Chancellor, George Osborne presented himself as 'George the Builder' and made regular appearances on construction sites throughout the country, complete with hard hat. 'We are the builders,' was George's battle cry throughout the 2014 party conference as he announced a number of initiatives to boost infrastructure and employment.

However, as you might expect from an expert in triangulation, the reality on the ground was different. All his major infrastructure projects relied heavily on huge amounts of construction aggregates sourced from quarries. HS2 alone would have required millions of tonnes of track ballast, sub-base, concrete and drainage materials; all made with aggregates and all subject to a stealth tax which few people had ever heard of, the Aggregates Levy. The Tories had fought the Aggregates Levy tooth and nail when it was introduced by Gordon Brown and had promised to repeal it; perhaps they forgot.

The Aggregates Levy was presented as an environmental tax to increase the use of recycled aggregates by increasing the price of virgin aggregates. £2 per tonne might not have seemed like much to the man in the street but it represented 50% price hike in less affluent regions. Not only did the UK quarry industry already lead every other European country in recycling, there was no significant environmental issue with quarries and no bulging file of complaints. Accordingly, no environmental gains or increased recycling ensued. Not only had the UK quarry industry been framed, it had been nationalised as well. Whether it was roads, railways, houses, bridges or hospitals, all were built using aggregates and all were charged the levy, plus VAT of course! Triangulation was the name of the game and it was a good one, for George the Builder that is.

Osborne made great play of devolving power to the regions and creating powerhouses to compete with London. In another of his speeches, the Chancellor referred to business rates which were set by central government, collected by councils and then redistributed by Whitehall across the country. Mr Osborne said this 'merry-go-round' would be ended, with local authorities retaining the proceeds locally and able to cut rates. What Mr Osborne failed to disclose was that local authorities would have their central funding cut to match. A problem passed on to others in the name of localism; Tony Blair would have been proud of him - as would Machiavelli.

However, politicians of all parties were susceptible to sharp-suited 'consultants' with glossy brochures selling systems or gizmos that often didn't work, were seldom value for money and often produced unintended consequences. Centralised computer systems was a hot favourite with countless billions being wasted in the NHS in particular but also in the DHSS and a failed attempt to roll out ID cards for all. Another classic was 'smart meters', which were set to cost consumers £11bn at a time when most people were reading their own meters anyway. The meters were made in China and the Chinese government could have used them at will to destabilise and crash the UK grid. Smart meters were presented as a means for people to save electricity both by becoming more aware of how much their appliances were using and by being able to benefit from off-peak rates. However, they also had another function which was not highlighted in the advertising. Power companies had known for some time that, due to the closure of so much base load coal-fired generation and the unreliable nature of renewable sources, trouble lay ahead. Major industrial consumers of electricity were already signed up to discount tariffs having agreed to be switched of during periods of shortage. However, with smart meters power suppliers now had the ability to charge premium rates at times of peak demand. Poorer people might now need to wait till off-peak times to eat or wash.

The imposition of differential rates of taxes used to have more to do with politics than revenue raising. Militant socialists wanted to punish the rich 'until the pips squeaked', while the wealthy wanted to, not so much squeeze the poor, as to preserve as much of their, often hard-earned, cash as possible. But with politics taken out of the equation, there was a truce in the class war and the level of taxation could be determined on more reasonable criteria.

The main recipients of this revenue were health insurance and pensions. Local services were still funded by local levies as this system had proved to be popular and fair. The cost of food and services had plummeted in line with the removal of grants for agriculture and the installation of modern high-efficiency power stations. The fuel bill for long-distance commuting was cut dramatically as local industries and local working flourished. Everyone knew that they were now in a much better place and the feel-good factor was strong. Financial pressures had not returned after the 2018 implosion and aspirations were now much more centred on happiness than wealth; it turned out the two were sometimes mutually exclusive after all. Not only did everyone look and feel better, but crime levels plummeted as society grew stronger and more inclusive. The effect of better quality education was also helping to turn out well adjusted, intelligent and aspirational young people with little interest in drugs or crime. The difference in hospital admissions was quite staggering. Not only had drink, drug and obesity-linked diseases decreased, but mental health issues had also receded. The number of people claiming disability benefits had also shrunk as everyone now wanted to play a part, no matter how limited. The old culture of devil take the hindmost with unaffordable rights being provided by paid hands had been transformed into a proud vigorous society supremely fit for purpose.

Self-Sufficiency in Food

Britain now made much better use its land and was self-sufficient in the supply of food. At a National Farmers' Union conference in February 2016, ahead of the Brexit vote, George Eustice, the UK's pro-Leave farming minister promised that farmers' subsidies would be safe if Britain left the EU. Eustice claimed that a portion of the £18billion dividend, resulting from a vote for Brexit, would go towards farming and protecting the environment through a continuing, UK-devised subsidy system. The government would do this 'without a shadow of a doubt', he claimed. Politicians were of course good at making promises beyond their power to fulfil. In the event, this decision was also taken out of politicians' hands as the cash to hand out to farmers disappeared along with everyone else's.

New Zealand had also been forced to scrap farm subsidies but the results surprised everyone, including their own farmers. After World War II, New Zealand was a highly successful agricultural nation with the second-highest per capita income in the world. The government was dominated by farmers with just about every minister being one.

However, before long the farmer-dominated NZ government began an ill-fated attempt to control the food market to benefit farming even more. It set up marketing boards to either limit or expand production and set prices. Flushed by its 'success', the government started imposing import tariffs and quotas on manufactured goods as well. The aim was to increase the prices of imports and make manufacturing in New Zealand more competitive. For a while this worked and 'Fortress New Zealand' had a good economy and little unemployment. But in putting up trade barriers NZ had sowed the seeds of disaster.

When Britain joined the EU in 1973 tariffs were placed on NZ imports to protect inefficient EU farmers. Shortly afterwards the rocketing price of oil fuelled inflation and the NZ economy began to crumble. In 1984 New Zealand experienced a major economic crisis. The NZ government, in a manner later repeated by the UK, had borrowed heavily and run huge deficits. Threatened with the loss of their subsidies, the farmers, rather than fighting a battle they would inevitably lose made the government an astonishing offer. They agreed to the loss of their subsidies, in the national interest, if the government scrapped all the other restrictive trade barriers as well.

The government duly did this but made the farmers go first and it was six years before the rest of the measures were fully implemented. Its lightly regulated economy quickly transformed NZ into one of the world's most successful trading nations.

NZ farming soon became a highly efficient market-led industry rather than one organised badly by the state. Before deregulation, NZ had 70m sheep and 50m lambs, many of which were rendered for fertiliser as there was no market for them. As a result they were only achieving a fraction of the price they could have by producing the high-quality sheep and lambs that the market wanted. Farmers also restricted their sheep farming to land fit for purpose. In the subsidised days sheep were often grazed on poor quality land just to keep the numbers up. Sheep numbers fell from seventy to forty million but the amount of meat sold remained the same. In addition, NZ farmers used much of the ground freed from sheep for other enterprises, notably dairy herds for butter and cheese production. Again high quality it even made its way onto UK shelves, despite having to pay the EU tariffs. However, NZ had to overcome more than just tariffs to access the EU market. When they developed butter that was spreadable straight from the fridge, EU officials banned it as it 'was not really butter'. However, such was the demand for this product that it was soon allowed in.

The New Zealand experience also demonstrated that food should always be grown where the climate and soil conditions are most suitable. Rather than subsidising farming on poor cold ground it makes more sense to import and spend the money saved on activities more suited to the local environment. This also provides a vital lifeline to producers in Third World countries and makes the world a much better place all round.

UK subsidies had long since disappeared along with the EU's disastrous Common Agricultural Policy but farmers responded by making every acre as productive as possible. The environment was still important but it was no longer going to trump the need for food. The vast landscapes of alien timber and sterile hillsides were quickly restored to a rich tapestry of mixed and sustainable agriculture blessed with a broad range of biodiversity. Even ground left empty since the Highland Clearances was repopulated with new settlements and hill farmers, well able to survive in a healthy organic market.

Before the Clearances, Highland crofters had been subsistence farmers and the landowners found it more profitable to turn the land over to sheep. But the demand for red meat in the UK had fallen – initially due to the fall in family income, then due to imports. The Common Agricultural Policy subsidies that had supported grouse moors were gone. Shooting was no longer the draw for the wealthy it once had been and opposition by animal rights activists had grown. It therefore made economic sense to return the Highlands to farmers producing high-value organic food.

A Beautiful Countryside for a Beautiful Nation

The physical appearance of the country was also different. The litter had disappeared and the potholes had been repaired. The wind farms were also gone, scrapped to reclaim their rare earth minerals and metals. Speculators who had been given twenty-five-year guaranteed income contracts were wiped out when the crash came and the subsidies stopped. Such was the intermittent and unreliable nature of these gigantic white elephants that they could not survive without massive subsidies and a guaranteed market. Once again political parties had sold us down the river to get votes, green votes. All recent governments had cynically exploited the green movement to get extra revenue. Gordon Brown and his acolyte Ed Balls kicked this process off in 1997 to get round their promise not to increase income and corporation taxes. Of course they were smart enough not to refer to them as taxes. The Climate Change Levy was applied to all households as well as major users of power. New Labour may have been experts at bending the truth to suit their own ends but they were not alone.

In recognition of their commercial potential, tourist areas had been given a thorough makeover and were now world class. Out-of-control road and trackside shrubbery and trees that had once enjoyed the unmerited protection of environmentalists were cut back to open up magnificent vistas and passing places, and viewpoints with proper facilities had been added. The hills, lakes and lochs were now presented in all their glory, visitors were well catered for and tourism was booming.

Cleaning up Energy

Britain was now self-sufficient in energy. State-owned and foreign utilities had been replaced by mutualised companies to supply electricity, gas and water. There was no longer any need to negotiate with different suppliers to get a better deal, as every customer was now a shareholder. Shale gas generators purred unobtrusively in the background and the earlier blackouts were a distant memory. However, Thorium reactors were also now in the pipeline and would replace shale to make carbon emissions lower still. Thorium was much more abundant than uranium but unlike uranium could not be used to produce weapons-grade plutonium which was why the much more dangerous uranium had long been favoured by governments. Thorium reactors could also be used to reprocess the plutonium and other nuclear waste from conventional reactors that the industry so badly needed to dispose of.

Healthcare & Education

The new Mutual Health Service – where its staff had a say in its governance – had become a valuable export in itself as foreign nationals came to the UK to access high-quality and affordable medical care. This also extended into care homes and day nurseries where families played a much more proactive role. In an interesting development a number of care homes and nurseries combined. The old folks got great fun and stimulus from the children and were delighted to help out where able with looking after them. Storytelling was a particular treat for young and old alike. Mutualism also flourished in education where cooperative schools drove up standards and the parents helped out with additional funding and extra-curricular activities. By now private schools had also disappeared as the new cooperative schools were every bit as good, if not better. Parents who might have used these exclusive schools in the past were much happier to have their children educated alongside others from their own community. Although most were relieved not to have to pay twice, the biggest bonus was that an inclusive education would lead to a more inclusive society for their children in the long term.

As a post-industrial country, the UK needed to produce high-value goods, so highly trained and highly skilled workers were much in demand. Britain was once again a world leader in education and the benefits to society, the economy and the future were immeasurable.

Global Nationalism

All over the world, patriotism and internationalism had replaced narrow nationalism.

The deeply troubled European Union had made way for a much more relaxed and informal union, underpinned by common consent rather than imposed by an ideological political elite. The old Eurozone was no more. After Greece had left, the other countries of southern Europe followed suit. Northern countries tried to cling on, but after France's economy faltered further, the Germans decided that they were no longer prepared to prop up the euro on their own and national currencies were reissued. The EU had failed spectacularly in political, economic, military and social terms but it was with a sense of great relief that nation states returned to their traditional ways. Older and poorer perhaps but a great deal wiser and happier.

The political ideal of a united Europe had failed most markedly during the refugee crisis when EU nations had failed to take military action against the Syrian regime. The EU did take many thousands of refugees but their generosity soon wilted in the face of fierce protests from their own people. Logic should have told the EU leaders that they couldn't have taken them all in any event and something would have to be done to tackle the problem in Syria, Afghanistan, Somalia et al.

It was Britain's prolonged Brexit negotiation that finally killed off the European Union. Although the UK voted narrowly to leave, referendums never settle anything. The Europhiles had not gone away and, along with Scottish separatists, were soon demanding a fresh plebiscite. However, once the Brexit vote failed to produce the predicted Armageddon, the mood had changed. UK negotiators adopted a tough stance and other nations began to demand similar terms. With twenty-eight countries all demanding treaty changes in their own national interest, the situation became impossible. The only thing they could agree on was the nullification of the treaties they had previously entered into. Local democracy returned but the borders remained open and its members at peace. After all was said and done, the value of peaceful cooperation and trade had been well-learned by the former member states.

The collapse of the EU had provided the ultimate vindication for George Orwell. The Scots had forgotten about their lost referendum for independence. There was no longer any need, now that they were 'independent' of state control and understood the true meaning of the word 'freedom.' Once the deregulation process was complete, centralised government in London and Edinburgh became minimal and decision-making was kept at the most local level possible. Something the EU had long promised but never delivered, subsidiarity. Parents were free to choose schools for their children or create their own; people with disabilities got to spend their own budget on provisions they set themselves.

In the developing world, the emphasis had changed from handouts to helping them gain the stability, the knowledge and the democratic autonomy required to catch up and take their place alongside other countries as equals. China was still active in Africa but it was now a balanced partnership of mutual benefit. China needed the raw materials that the African nations could provide and it had plenty of foreign exchange to spend.

The rich nations found that it was no longer acceptable to exploit cheap labour in developing countries as well-informed consumers now shunned goods produced in sweatshops. Companies in the developed world also realised that it did little good to keep workers in developing countries on starvation wages when they needed emerging markets to export to.

Immigration: Rebalancing the Ethnic Scales

In Britain the demographics were also changing, much to the satisfaction of all concerned. As the country returned to an even keel, many expatriates came home and entire families were reunited. Although the older generation had been stoic at their offspring having to seek their fortunes elsewhere, nothing could conceal their joy when they came back. This had seldom happened before as the vast majority of those who had emigrated felt no desire to return to a country which was in terminal decline. Not only that, but many of the immigrants who had come to Britain to escape poverty or oppression in their native countries were packing up to return home as well. Even second and third-generation immigrants had never lost their homing instincts or their traditions. Not only were their own countries now developing fast, with jobs aplenty, but the climate was also a consideration not to be ignored. Given the sheer amount of immigration that had taken place since 1997, this exodus had a major effect on the price and availability of housing. Young people could at last find homes they could afford and quickly made the most of this unexpected bonus.

A Blissful Dawn

Robert Burns told us that 'a man's a man for all that' but we failed to appreciate the depth of this sentiment. The gurgling laugh of an innocent child is the same in any language but the significance of this also escaped us. It took a long time for us to realise that self-reliance, moral responsibility and a respect for others were the only 'weapons' that were needed to allow mankind to live in harmony. And that was the prospect for 2024.

Robert Burns 1795
Then let us pray that come it may,
(As come it will for a' that,)
That Sense and Worth, o'er a' the earth,
Shall bear the gree, an' a' that.
For a' that, an' a' that,
It's coming yet for a' that,
That Man to Man, the world o'er,
Shall brothers be for a' that.

New Initiatives Introduced in 2024
International Court of Human Rights www.ichr.global
Project Peace www.project peace.global
Free Parliament www.freeparliament.org.uk
Unintended Consequences www.unintended.wiki
Voting Platforms www.voteEngland.org & www.voteScotland.org